Kitten Licks

33 1/3 Global

33 1/3 Global, a series related to but independent from **33 1/3**, takes the format of the original series of short, music-based books and brings the focus to music throughout the world. With initial volumes focusing on Japanese and Brazilian music, the series will also include volumes on the popular music of Australia/Oceania, Europe, Africa, the Middle East, and more.

33 1/3 Japan

Series Editor: Noriko Manabe

Spanning a range of artists and genres—from the 1970s rock of Happy End to technopop band Yellow Magic Orchestra, the Shibuya-kei of Cornelius, classic anime series *Cowboy Bebop*, J-Pop/EDM hybrid Perfume, and vocaloid star Hatsune Miku—33 1/3 Japan is a series devoted to in-depth examination of Japanese popular music of the twentieth and twenty-first centuries.

Published Titles:

Supercell's *Supercell* by Keisuke Yamada

AKB48 by Patrick W. Galbraith and Jason G. Karlin

Yoko Kanno's *Cowboy Bebop Soundtrack* by Rose Bridges

Perfume's *Game* by Patrick St. Michel

Cornelius's *Fantasma* by Martin Roberts

Joe Hisaishi's *My Neighbor Totoro: Soundtrack* by Kunio Hara

Shonen Knife's *Happy Hour* by Brooke McCorkle

Nenes' *Koza Dabasa* by Henry Johnson

Yuming's *The 14th Moon* by Lasse Lehtonen

Forthcoming Titles:

Yellow Magic Orchestra's *Yellow Magic Orchestra* by Toshiyuki Ohwada

Kohaku utagassen: The Red and White Song Contest by Shelley Brunt

Toshiko Akiyoshi-Lew Tabackin Big Band's *Kogun* by E. Taylor Atkins

S.O.B.'s *Don't Be Swindle* by Mahon Murphy and Ran Zwigenberg

33 1/3 Brazil

Series Editor: Jason Stanyek

Covering the genres of samba, tropicália, rock, hip hop, forró, bossa nova, heavy metal and funk, among others, 33 1/3 Brazil is a series devoted to in-depth examination of the most important Brazilian albums of the twentieth and twenty-first centuries.

Published Titles:

Caetano Veloso's *A Foreign Sound* by Barbara Browning

Tim Maia's *Tim Maia Racional Vols. 1 &2* by Allen Thayer

João Gilberto and Stan Getz's *Getz/Gilberto* by Brian McCann

Gilberto Gil's *Refazenda* by Marc A. Hertzman

Dona Ivone Lara's *Sorriso Negro* by Mila Burns

Milton Nascimento and Lô Borges's *The Corner Club* by Jonathon Grasse

Racionais MCs' *Sobrevivendo no Inferno* by Derek Pardue

Naná Vasconcelos's *Saudades* by Daniel B. Sharp

Chico Buarque's First *Chico Buarque* by Charles A. Perrone

Forthcoming Titles:

Jorge Ben Jor's *África Brasil* by Frederick J. Moehn

33 1/3 Europe

Series Editor: Fabian Holt

Spanning a range of artists and genres, 33 1/3 Europe offers engaging accounts of popular and culturally significant albums of Continental Europe and the North Atlantic from the twentieth and twenty-first centuries.

Published Titles:

Darkthrone's *A Blaze in the Northern Sky* by Ross Hagen

Ivo Papazov's *Balkanology* by Carol Silverman

Heiner Müller and Heiner Goebbels's *Wolokolamsker Chaussee* by Philip V. Bohlman

Modeselektor's *Happy Birthday!* by Sean Nye
Mercyful Fate's *Don't Break the Oath* by Henrik Marstal
Bea Playa's *I'll Be Your Plaything* by Anna Szemere and András Rónai
Various Artists' *DJs do Guetto* by Richard Elliott
Czesław Niemen's *Niemen Enigmatic* by Ewa Mazierska and Mariusz Gradowski
Massada's *Astaganaga* by Lutgard Mutsaers
Los Rodriguez's *Sin Documentos* by Fernán del Val and Héctor Fouce
Édith Piaf's *Récital 1961* by David Looseley
Nuovo Canzoniere Italiano's *Bella Ciao* by Jacopo Tomatis
Iannis Xenakis's *Persepolis* by Aram Yardumian
Vopli Vidopliassova's *Tantsi* by Maria Sonevytsky
Amália Rodrigues's *Amália at the Olympia* by Lila Ellen Gray
Ardit Gjebrea's *Projekt Jon* by Nicholas Tochka

Forthcoming Titles:
J.M.K.E.'s *To the Cold Land* by Brigitta Davidjants
Taco Hemingway's *Jarmark* by Kamila Rymajdo
Tripes' *Kefali Gemato Hrisafi* by Dafni Tragaki
Silly's *Februar* by Michael Rauhut

33 1/3 Oceania

Series Editors: Jon Stratton (senior editor) and Jon Dale (specialising in books on albums from Aotearoa/New Zealand)
Spanning a range of artists and genres from Australian Indigenous artists to Maori and Pasifika artists, from Aotearoa/New Zealand noise music to Australian rock, and including music from Papua and other Pacific islands, 33 1/3 Oceania offers exciting accounts of albums that illustrate the wide range of music made in the Oceania region.

Published Titles:
John Farnham's *Whispering Jack* by Graeme Turner
The Church's *Starfish* by Chris Gibson
Regurgitator's *Unit* by Lachlan Goold and Lauren Istvandity
Kylie Minogue's *Kylie* by Adrian Renzo and Liz Giuffre

Kitten Licks

Ben Green and Ian Rogers

Series Editors: Jon Stratton, UniSA Creative, University of South Australia, and Jon Dale, University of Melbourne, Australia

BLOOMSBURY ACADEMIC

NEW YORK • LONDON • OXFORD • NEW DELHI • SYDNEY

BLOOMSBURY ACADEMIC
Bloomsbury Publishing Inc
1385 Broadway, New York, NY 10018, USA
50 Bedford Square, London, WC1B 3DP, UK
29 Earlsfort Terrace, Dublin 2, Ireland

BLOOMSBURY, BLOOMSBURY ACADEMIC and the Diana logo are
trademarks of Bloomsbury Publishing Plc

First published in the United States of America 2024

A catalog record for this book is available from the Library of Congress.

ISBN: HB: 978-1-5013-9328-0
          PB: 978-1-5013-9329-7
          ePDF: 978-1-5013-9331-0
          eBook: 978-1-5013-9330-3

Series: 33 1/3 Oceania

Typeset by Integra Software Services Pvt. Ltd.
Printed and bound in Great Britain

To find out more about our authors and books visit www.bloomsbury.
com and sign up for our newsletters.

BEN

For Angus

IAN

For Kate, Ross, Marieca and Nicola.

Contents

1 Static from the Stars

An Introduction

Australian music TV has always been a strange beast. Since *Six O'Clock Rock* in 1959, the Australian Broadcasting Corporation (ABC) – the country's BBC or PBS – have provided popular music programming. A distinctively Australian approach began in the 1970s with *Countdown*, a haphazard, at-times chaotic viewing experience, hosted by the dazed and bumbling Molly Meldrum.[1] That energy continued with the durable late-night *rage*, a weekend 'host-less' or 'guest-programmed' clip show starting in the late 1980s. *rage* is a vast programme, more a national exhibition of the ABC vaults than any sort of peg for music marketing. Every video is played on *rage*, from the classic to the pornographic, DIY produced to high end. Yet even for the Australian viewership – an audience steeped in these eccentricities – the mid-90s incarnation of this energy, a show called *Recovery*, proved a wild ride. *Recovery*'s host Dylan Lewis came off as aggressively unprofessional – Molly Meldrum squared: sly, ironic, disinterested, almost embarrassed by his role – and the show around him gave off a chaotic, gonzo energy: elaborate sets were destroyed, celebrity interviews were derailed and an impossibly broad assortment of musicians performed, everyone from Sonic Youth and Public Enemy through to the local band down the road. This all happened in real-time on a tax-payer-funded live broadcast every Saturday morning.

Very quickly, *Recovery* became emblematic of a specific moment in Australian music – the grunge-led 90s wherein there was a changing of the guard in rock'n'roll. Polished was out. Grit was in. Noise was in. Loud-soft-loud was the songwriting template. In 1996, Brisbane rock three-piece Screamfeeder performed on the show. They encapsulated much of this. Screamfeeder were there to promote their album *Kitten Licks*, their fourth since forming in 1991.

As was customary on *Recovery* the band played two songs, starting with album opener 'Static'. To watch them on *Recovery* is to see a band tentatively taking steps into the limelight, emphasis on *tentatively*. 'Static' is restrained this morning, performed carefully, knowing full well what it is: a potential hit, in need of promotion. 'Static' opens on a descending lead line accompanied by a long, 5-second snare roll, before cutting to Tim Steward's coarse vocal:

> *I'm going to build a radio*
> *With static from the stars*

It's a song about a mythical radio station, based on a story Tim read in an American fanzine. Impressionistic from start to finish, 'Static' is hard to grasp. Partly an ode to the chance and magic of radio broadcasting (it will soon become the de facto anthem of the band's hometown community radio station 4ZZZ), it also shouts out to a very 90s trope: the valorisation of obscurity.

> *I'm going to call it nothing because you don't need to be known*
> *My signal will get lost in all the white noise floating by*
> *It drifts above the cities invisible in the sky*

Singing this on national TV is no joke for the band's Tim Steward, though. His voice is a melodic punk voice – more Bob Mould than Kurt Cobain, to cite the moment, with an accent floating in the mid-Atlantic centre of the genre – and getting it right involves a degree of standing still and hitting the cues.

The camera zooms in around his head (his cropped sandy hair), wherein the whole country can count five ear-rings in his right lobe. It's a look.

Stage left is Kellie Lloyd on bass guitar. Kellie isn't moving a great deal either, but the camera finds her often: she's wearing the classic 90s combo of long-sleeve tee under short-sleeve tee and her hair is long and dreadlocked. To the unaccustomed viewer, this no doubt reads as some sort of exotic tropical Queensland hippiedom – a very hazy, bong-water-tinged vision of the Australian north – but in reality, it's Swervedriver cosplay. Kellie would later describe her look as the bizarro Adam Franklin, 'the white girl version', and if it ever looked awkward, it doesn't now. Somehow, it looks exactly like Brisbane in the middle of the 1990s.

Behind both of them is the band's new drummer, Dean Shwereb. Dean is inarguably the star of this performance. There's a lot of him on-screen and the details presented are curious. Firstly, he's really working at it – hitting like he's still in his previous band: the sludgy metal outfit Hateman – but he's dressed in an orange vee-necked sweater, like a member of Belle and Sebastian. He has one of those professional drum kits that sit within a steel frame.

And yet the performance collides into a cohesive outpouring. 'Static' goes over well and the footage taken is good enough and clear enough to be edited into the official film clip for the song. Watching it now, twenty-five years later on YouTube, it typifies the mood of 1996 in Brisbane. Here was a rock three-piece, singing a song about isolation and obscurity to the nation. It's no lost signal, though. It was a message beamed into hundreds of thousands of households and it said as much about the state of the Australian music industry as anything else. Things were changing. A band like

Screamfeeder could be going places. There was an undeniable energy to it. A hopeful spark. And yet, and yet …

Screamfeeder played another track from *Kitten Licks* that day, a song called 'Bridge Over Nothing'. It's the second song on the album and it's as bracing as 'Static', providing *Kitten Licks* with a vital one-two punch. Yet 'Bridge Over Nothing' has an altogether darker tone. It's chaotic where 'Static' is controlled. It is hectic, noisy and bittersweet. Dean's blasting drum work is pure Keith Moon – all snare and cymbals – and the opening pattern is held for impossibly long measures: throughout the introduction, verse and half the chorus. In the din, Tim's voice is stretched, bringing out all the strange and necessary punk elongations required to stay in time and tune. The verse lyrics are dictates, a list of notes-to-self:

> *Don't talk about what you thought about alone …*
> *Don't think about what you heard was true before …*
> *Don't be scared by laws that keep you in your lanes …*
> *Don't be cornered by the corners in your mind …*

But then something remarkable happens in the chorus of 'Bridge Over Nothing' and the impact of it is caught full-force on the *Recovery* broadcast. The band enter the chorus. Dean shifts the drumming, slowly finding a straighter rhythm, and then Kellie steps up. Up until this point, Kellie has been primarily tasked with holding the song together. Her bass line is like a rope through the middle of the thing, but halfway into the chorus – *halfway* – she starts to sing:

> *Bridge going nowhere over nothing.*
> *Bridge going nowhere over nothing.*

This happens exactly as Dean finds time, as Tim pushes his voice further and it is – and always has been, ever since – a type of indie-rock miracle, travelling from abject chaos to locked-in rock catharsis in an instant. The song's unlikely yet economical structure, along with its breathless, precise execution, could only be the product of countless hours playing together. It's muscle memory and on *Recovery* the band flex. They're not poised or careful with 'Bridge Over Nothing'. They flail around. Tim jumps in the air. Kellie whirls in circles. The track pours out of them. This happens because it *is* them. They're on national television, on this crazy TV show, playing over the closing credits as the set is destroyed around them, but everything their hometown knows about their live show is on full display because 'Bridge Over Nothing' is so comfortable, so Screamfeeder. They transcend their context with *this*, not 'Static', and the contrast between these two songs provides a telling moment. It was there for everyone to see.

…

On *Kitten Licks*, 'Static' and 'Bridge Over Nothing' overlap, tied together by a strand of feedback. A few minutes later, the second song's final chord rings out over the distinctive opening beat of 'Dart', another single and possibly Screamfeeder's best-known and loved song. In fact, all of the tracks, barring a side break, are smooshed together with no silence between them ('I don't like gaps on records,' says Tim). It's one of the album's charms, a kind of meta-hook, adding to its qualities of dynamism and abundance ('The songs are so strong and they just keep coming,' says fan and musician Kate Cooper). It also parallels the story of *Kitten Licks*. Not only as the fourth album in five years from a restless, relentless working band, written in a collective hot streak, recorded and mixed in a flash ('The way the songs overlap, that was just done on the fly as well,' says Tim). But also as an album of incongruous contiguities, *Kitten*

Licks is not so much a crossover as an intersection, representing in various ways a meeting point, a high-water mark, and a transition – for Screamfeeder and for the worlds around them. That is the story told in this book.

The story, like most, takes *place*. Screamfeeder have been a Brisbane band since that label was a novelty. With *Kitten Licks* they were one of the 'big four' that drew eyes and ears to the once provincial, but increasingly worldly Queensland capital, along with Custard, Powderfinger and Regurgitator. Leading up to that point, as a mural at Fortitude Valley railway station now recalls, 'Screamfeeder set a precedent in being content to remain at home', instead of making the usual move to Sydney, Melbourne or London to build on early successes.[2] *Kitten Licks* is a product of shared rehearsal rooms and crowded music venues in grimy but lively Fortitude Valley. This was the early phase of the inner city suburb's transition, from seedy hub of illegal casinos and brothels (and the corrupt police who profited from them for decades before Queensland's late 1980s political seachange), to gentrified nightlife and entertainment precinct. The album is equally a product of the band members' domestic lives and creative solitude in humid sharehouses and flats, dotted across the still-cheap, leafy inner west just a few steep hills or sharp riverbends away. However, Brisbane wasn't always home.

Screamfeeder have a regional Queensland backstory (some *Kitten Licks* press still calls them a Townsville band), and Tim's musical identity was taking shape even earlier in 1980s punk London. This helps explain something about their sound: Tim's accent and the music itself blend pop, punk and grunge, remaining untethered to any one place and summoning instead the made-up, mediated cosmos of modern music (static from the stars). Kellie Lloyd is both an insider and outsider: at home in Brisbane's music scene (when Tim arrives), but not from there either, a woman in a male-dominated world, and endlessly restless as a person. All this might explain why the band is so at home on the road. Screamfeeder spent the 1990s touring – before *Kitten Licks*, driving nearly 1,000 kilometres to Sydney every other month – and then after *Kitten Licks*, expanding to coastal and inland regional towns like the ones they all grew up in ('A lot of driving, a lot of flying,' says Dean). When asked in interviews about the rising 'Brisbane scene', the band members would point out that they were hardly there, feeling more kinship with the artists they saw all the time on tour. This family of bands – including Melbourne's Spiderbait, Geelong's Magic Dirt, Sydney's You Am I and several of Screamfeeder's Brisbane peers – came, with the aid of national youth media and festivals, to represent a 'homegrown' Australian alternative to both US grunge and UK Britpop. Meanwhile, there were Screamfeeder's ill-fated ambitions in the United States, which began before *Kitten Licks* but loomed again in the wake of its Australian success, indelibly shaping the band's mid-career arc.

This story, like most, also happens upon a time: essentially, in Australia's dream of the Nineties. As we will see, 1996 is a critical year, with new festivals (including an all-Australian line-up for the Homebake festival) and media (including *Recovery* and the national expansion of the ABC's youth radio network Triple J) capturing, and to some extent creating, a trans-local Australian music scene with an expanding, all-ages audience. This coincides with the increasing merger of the country's independent and major record label networks, sending members of Screamfeeder's musical family to the top of the charts. *Kitten Licks*, with fully independent distribution, would not climb as high as some, but its release in August is right on the tip of a cresting wave, capturing this generational energy just before it breaks. It was certainly a breakthrough for the band, who rode the wave all the way to the strange shores of a new century. 'Everything was happening, and it wasn't happening *to* us 'cause we were creating it, but … it just did become this thing that was happening to us,' says Kellie.

Last, and far from least, this story has lessons. In making *Kitten Licks*, Screamfeeder – in their fifth (or arguably ninth) year, on their fourth album, with a brand-new drummer – learnt how to be the band they've been for decades to follow, personally and creatively. Writing this book has brought lessons for us too. We thought this would be a story about what could have been and almost was: *Kitten Licks* as a missed smash hit and an underrated classic (which, for many, is part of its appeal). In short, we anticipated a story about surviving a type of commercial/cultural failure, with all the attendant troubles, and Screamfeeder as resilient subjects of fate and circumstance. A tragedy, of sorts. But what we documented in our interviews and research presents a very different narrative, one focused on sustainability, friendship and survival. It turns out to be a tale of what was chosen and how far it leads: *Kitten Licks* as a testament to the potential of independent music-making, with Screamfeeder as stalwart pursuers of artistic control and personal longevity. This, in turn, finally explains the respect and influence the band enjoy among multiple generations of musicians and fans, and the ubiquitous love for this album. Screamfeeder and *Kitten Licks* show what is possible, how to do it – and how to keep on doing it.

In this book, the story of *Kitten Licks* is told by the people who lived it, and who still do. The band members, the record producer, peers and fans, journalists, and more, in their own words, then and now (for context about the people quoted, see the *Cast of Characters* at the end of the book). We began these conversations during a period of reflection, just after the thirtieth anniversary of the band and the twenty-fifth anniversary of *Kitten Licks*. Screamfeeder played the album in full, in a double-header with Regurgitator performing *Tu-Plang*, and sold stacks of a new vinyl in the process. A documentary film about Screamfeeder is in production, and the band themselves have published a photo memoir called *End of This Summer* (2022), alongside an album-by-album podcast series titled *The Ending Goes Forever* (2022). And they're not the only ones revisiting their legacy. Screamfeeder are once again sharing luridly coloured bills with Custard, Magic Dirt, Spiderbait, Tumbleweed and You Am I, for nostalgia-fests attended by many of the same punters who saw them three decades ago. Who said don't look back? But as we wrote this book, Screamfeeder also released their eighth album, *Five Rooms*. They launched it at a national run of shows with support from Adalita (of Magic Dirt) – just six months on from the 'Screamfeeder – Since 1991' thirtieth anniversary tour, where their epic sets of crowd-pleasing deep cuts were supported by up-and-comers like Brisbane's Mouse. Tim and Kellie also played as solo artists and with other bands, including Tim's We All Want To, and Kellie's Majestic Horses and Deafcult. They are semi-professional musicians, with creative day jobs. We found them at a unique moment in time, one where the band appeared actively interested in both their past and their future.

2 Madmen to Screamfeeder

Before *Kitten Licks*

Once seen as a provincial 'small town', Brisbane City was on the make in the early 1990s. Three million people lived in the state of Queensland, and half of that population resided in the city. Thus, the members of Screamfeeder shared an archetypal characteristic found in many Brisbane musicians of the time: they were not from there. Yet the only creatives who moved to Brisbane – instead of Sydney or Melbourne – were those who could imagine and daydream of central Brisbane as 'the big smoke'. There is something fundamentally different about the scale of one's desires when Brisbane serves as this frame of reference. Thus, at the start of the 90s, the Brisbane music scene was filled with people who had already made a move, but as the Nirvana-led alternative rock boom found its way to Australia, these same musicians all had to contend with the rapidly expanding horizons the moment wrought. For Screamfeeder, what started out as teenage affect and sharehouse fun, soon became a serious art project. Woven into this project was a huge amount of unspoken ambition – in keeping with the era – something that would ultimately drive the band forward, through the tricky terrain of their early albums.

Joe Woolley (Screamfeeder's current manager): For a band making their fourth record [in *Kitten Licks*], you can hear the confidence there and it's the confidence to do stuff that's still unconventional now. You would not have been allowed to make that record on a major label, they wouldn't have put up with it. Whatever they did with *Kitten Licks*, it's completely … The songs are really worked out to the last degree. Like, fuck, there's a lot of planning in that. You don't arrive at that by accident. So whatever was going on in their heads prior to that would be very interesting, 'cause it takes a great deal of self-confidence and a certain amount of stubbornness to insist on making a record like that. It's just not conventional. No, it's quite unconventional in many ways.

Tim Steward (Guitars, Vocals)

Tim: I grew up in England on a steady diet of Buddy Holly, Joseph and the Amazing Technicolour Dreamcoat and The Beatles, immediately followed by punk rock. When I was fifteen, my mum allowed me to go out to gigs in London, and back then it didn't matter about the whole alcohol thing. No one gave a shit if kids went into venues basically, and ordered pints of beer and that kind of thing. So me and my friend, we'd catch the train into the city and go out to see all these hardcore bands in the early Eighties. It was mind-blowing because you were suddenly in this sweaty venue full of punked out dudes in leather and spikes and mohawks and shit like that.

Joe Woolley: Tim's immensely likeable. It would be unfair to say that he has no ego, but he's really skilled at hiding it. He doesn't let it get in the way of doing what he needs to do. And he's a very self-aware person, which is a great attribute. He has a great knack of making the people that he meets feel important and feel that they can do things that he can't do. That he probably could do himself, if he wanted to put his mind to it, but he didn't want to. So he could get you to do stuff for him because you just liked him so much. He's easy to talk to and he's a person of the highest integrity. Tim doesn't badmouth people behind their back or say one thing to you and say one thing to someone else. He's incredibly straight, so if you were friends with Tim, you were friends with the real Tim.

Kellie Lloyd (bass guitar): He looked like a rock God kind of thing in the 90s, you know like very tall, blonde hair. Very friendly then, and he's still the same. He kind of makes everybody feel like they're the most important person to talk to. Like, he'd make a great politician. He probably won't remember your name.

Kellie Lloyd (Bass, Vocals)

Kellie: I was a weirdo at school, a loner. I didn't really fit in. I was an overachiever in lots of ways. I learnt how to play guitar early at eleven, then started a band at fourteen in Toowoomba when I got my first bass.[1] I came to Brisbane to go to film school and left my guitar behind for a while. There were a couple of people there who were into music. I eventually got my gear down to Brisbane and answered a few ads and went and jammed with people.

Joe: I have enormous regard for Kellie. She is again a person of the highest integrity, but insomuch as Tim is the kind of puppy dog running up and going 'pat me', Kellie is vastly more reserved. So you will earn Kellie's trust. Tim will trust you to do whatever you say you're gonna do. Kellie will wait and see whether you do it, before she kind of opens up her real self to you. It's just a different type of personality. Nothing wrong with it. She probably has to have a little bit of a tough exterior, being a woman in the music industry for that period of time. So Kellie is more reserved and you gotta prove yourself to her. You've gotta explain what you're gonna do, why you're gonna do it that way, how you're gonna do it, how you're gonna measure whether you've done it. And she's super smart and she knows when someone's talking shit, and she knows when you're talking about things you know about. I remember meeting her and having coffee with her and walking away going, I'm scared of her and I don't think she likes me.

Kellie: I was making lots of friends with all these people in bands and they'd come and stay at the house that I lived in. So I felt like my role was the Brisbane diplomat, if that's the right word – the consulate to Brisbane. It's like, *Welcome, I'll take you out and show you the Target building and Mount Coot-tha.* [2]

Tim: Just a real go-getter. I guess I thought she was pretty confident and, you know, really enmeshed in the scene, very important in the scene. And a real cool person to be honest, as well, like she had dreads and all that kind of stuff and, there were tonnes of people like that back then, plus she was a skater. So it was another sort of like entry for us into the scene really, meeting Kellie, because she might have felt it was the other way around, like she was putting herself in places, but we felt it was us getting embedded in the scene more as well, yeah.

Kellie: The other bands that I was in, I kind of wanted them to be long-term things, but I didn't know what to do. But I saw that Tim did. Like, you know, together Tim and Tony [Blades, former Screamfeeder drummer] were so ambitious, but not in a bad, evil way. They were just ambitious in this way, they just wanted to play gigs. They wanted to do it like American hardcore bands, like just touring, get in the car, just fucking go, just drive and play shows. And I was like, that's what I want to do. And so, the three of us, it was just this magic kind of thing and then when Dean joined it was like, a better bunch of people, like a better personality fit.

Dean Shwereb (Drums)

Dean: I started getting into hip hop in Mackay, of all places.[3] In high school, I was just a quiet dude. We moved to Tewantin and I started getting into skateboarding and then when I was in Year 11, I broke my arm.[4] After that, I said *I'm not a skateboarder anymore*. My dad was a drummer and I asked him if he'd set up a drum kit for me. I think the first track I listened to was 'Hells Bells' by AC/DC. And I said *Yeah I can do this*.

Joe: Dean is just super personable. Super fun. You know, the kind of guy that, things come out of his mouth and you're just going, 'What the fuck are you talking about?' 'Cause he'd just come out with these sayings and I can't recall them, but you just sit there and when you stop laughing, you go *What the fuck?* So he's quirky and very funny and an amazing drummer.

Tim: He's so amazing and he's so confident and upright.

Starting Out and Coming Together

Tim: When I was sixteen, I moved from England to Australia. I moved to Townsville, this tiny little tropical town, and it was a very different scene.[5] I knew I wanted to form a band. After I finished Year 12, I moved back to England for nine months to live with my dad and I hung out with some friends from school and bought an electric guitar off a friend of mine. I brought it back to Townsville and moved out of home. I was on the dole, living in share-houses, drinking and smoking pot. I met some people at the local radio station called Triple T and started putting a band together. About four months later, I met Tony. We hired him through a newspaper ad. He was fifteen and he joined the band and we changed name to The Madmen. That was in '87. By late '88, we hopped in the van and went to Brissy. We made it to Brisbane about three times before moving here. It was really the punk scene that we went to and they kind of embraced us. We felt like we were in a bigger place, so we sort of upped our game a little, and went to practice a lot. Tony was always booking the band, we'd play two times every weekend, all the time. There were venues everywhere and heaps of bands. And it was like Townsville 'cause everyone was on the dole and they could afford to do it, so they had tonnes of time to put into music.

Kellie: I found a couple of people that I liked and started a band called November Bled. The drummer from that band was from Townsville, he knew these guys called The Madmen, and we got a couple of shows with them. I had to make a film clip in my second year at film school so I wrote a letter to The Madmen and said *Can I make a film clip for you?* Also, at this time, I was playing in a band called Krud which was made up of all these film students like James Lees and Jeff Graham who later became Hateman. So I contacted Tim from The Madmen, told him who I was, that we'd played together and he said 'I've heard you've got a really good practice room, could we move in?' It was my house, but they did. A year later, after them practising weekly, they kicked their bass player out and Krud broke up and I joined The Madmen.

Flour (1992)

Tim: We'd been writing and recording [as The Madmen] for three or four years by then. So we had the momentum up and running. Kellie just hopped on board the train. We already had maybe a dozen songs we were ready to record. So we just hit the studio and did it within two months.[6] We recorded it in Brisbane, mostly at a studio called Vibrafeel, in the beautiful suburb of Inala.[7] It was recorded from November '91 through to January '92. It was great, but at the time because we moved so fast, we barely appreciated what we had with Kellie. She's frickin' amazing, but we were just like, *Here's another song to learn. We're going on tour next week*, and we didn't stop to look around and say this is really cool, even though in retrospect, it obviously was.

Kellie: We played a show as The Madmen – I think it was at The Story Bridge Hotel – and then we changed the name to Screamfeeder. We were recording [Screamfeeder's 1992 debut album] *Flour* at that stage already, and some demo cassettes were sent off.

Tom Morgan (musician): It must have cost the band a small fortune in postage because I remember every man and his dog having a copy of that cassette. I lifted mine from the *Half a Cow* shop. [8]

Kellie: We signed to [indie label] Survival in Sydney, and then we started touring and it all went nuts!

Tom Morgan: When *Flour* was released it was obvious just how ahead of the curve 'the 'feeder' were. While most of us were still trying to figure out how to write a tune, the songs on *Flour* had structure, wit, melody and dynamics. It became an instant fixture on my new '5 disc carousel CD changer'. So much so, that later when the stereo was stolen, *Flour* went with it. [9]

Andrew Stafford (journalist and author): For almost any Brisbane band before them, it would have been time to move on. But Screamfeeder set a precedent in being content to remain at home.[10]

Tim: Brisbane at the time was very open, very free and really fertile, music-wise, for sure. There were a number of different scenes who would all touch each other and rub shoulders, you know there was the punk scene, and there was this little grunge-ish scene that we were a part of, and those scenes would definitely overlap here and there, there'd be gigs with bands from each scene. There'd even be metal bands, or bands like Pangaea, and they were more like, I dread to say the word funk but it had that more, maybe sort of Chili Peppers-ish bass-led vibe. And at the same time there were a whole lot of bands who were in the lo-fi indie pop, shoegazey, kinda twee scene. There were just so many gigs, all the time, and you could go out three or four nights a week, which is what you did at that age. We'd see all the same friends, there was a real community actually, and that was the lovely thing about it.[11]

Dean: When I first moved to Brisbane, Screamfeeder were everywhere. You know, they were always playing gigs. You would pick up a street mag and – bang! – they were in your face every week. My friends and I would slag them off. I was jealous. I wanted to be in the band.

Tim: In Brisbane in the Nineties, everyone was on the dole and it was so cheap to live. It made life really easy, 'cause rent was always so much cheaper than Sydney and Melbourne. You'd be going around the country on tour, putting your form in everywhere and living like a king, basically. I don't know what young kids do anymore, if they're not working I don't know how they survive really. 'Cause that really enabled us to be in a band and be a working band. Otherwise we would have been slowed down heaps.

Dean: I met Paul [Service, Hateman guitarist] in the line at the DSS [Department of Social Security] of all places. You know, you'd be handing in your forms. I was unemployed for ages, I didn't know what I was doing. And he said, *Oh man, we're looking for a drummer dude, do you wanna come on tour?* And that was a tour with [Chicago band] Shellac. He must have just known some people that I knew. I said, *Yeah absolutely*, jumped in the van and pretty much off we went.

Damien Hughes (fan): When you're that young like I was at that time, you've got a youthful enthusiasm where you are so into music, music means the world to you, nothing can take that away from you. But the only band that I ever really had a very personal connection to was Screamfeeder. And that's because of the people they were. If I sent Tim a letter, the following week there would be a letter back in my letterbox. I didn't have that connection with any other band that I wrote to, and I wrote to a lot of bands.

Kellie: I'd fuck things up all the time. At gigs I'd always forget stuff. I was drinking. There were lots of times where I would mess shit up at practise and, there were probably times where everyone was like, *she can't do this*. But I did. We toured for years and years. We'd always come back, because Tony had a day job. But we were always in the car, we'd drive everywhere, every weekend for years.

Burn Out Your Name (1993–4)

Kellie: In 1993 we drove to Sydney in Tim's van, to record our second album *Burn Out Your Name* [1993]. I was driving around and I barely had my license and it was so hard to drive that car.

Tim: It was March of '93. We recorded it in a studio called Megaphon in Sydney. We recorded and mixed in one session. And I literally remember when [producer] David Price would turn his back, I'd sneak up to the desk and drop the vocal level and push the guitar levels up. The singing is really buried.

Kellie: And also when you and he weren't looking, I was pushing the bass. And then Tony wouldn't know what to do, but he would ask to have the toms and the snare up, and so everyone was just battling for room in that record. [12]

Tim: After *Flour* we got fairly popular. *Burn Out Your Name* was more again. Tony and I were living together in Brisbane, in a suburb called Milton, on a road called Heussler Terrace, in this big share-house with us and our girlfriends. And we just seemed to be on this increasingly fast treadmill of activity. We weren't being bossed around by anyone, we were just excited and working hard, working fast, playing lots. We were going to practice probably three or four times a week, and learning new songs, and we just had a really good dynamic within the band. We could really push through a lot of songs really quickly.

Kellie: We were trying to assert ourselves. We were being picked up by Triple J [the ABC's youth-oriented radio network, which expanded its coverage nationally in the 1990s]. We were a bit of an *it* band. We were supporting all of the overseas bands that were coming out. And I know that when I wrote the bass lines for *Burn Out Your Name*, I just wanted to be the best bass player in Australia. I wanted to be better than every guy I'd ever met. I was very competitive but people probably didn't even really know that. I would never admit to it. But listening back to that record now, my God! I mean they're really good bass lines, but I was really a frustrated lead guitarist playing the bass. 'Cause I'd gone from playing the guitar to playing the bass, I wanted to fill out the sound. I just wanted to create something bigger than just playing single bass lines or whatever. I was really driven to be really good.

Jamie Hutchings (musician): *Burn Out Your Name* has everything that was special about the band during this era. [13]

Tim: Around *Burn Out Your Name*, we had a discussion with rooArt but me and Tony at the time were so like anti-major we just basically blew them off, you know? We kind of foiled ourselves at every available opportunity. [14]

Kellie: We said no. I remember it really well. Todd Wagstaff [rooArt A&R representative] came up to Brisbane, took us out to lunch, was wining and dining us in that way or whatever. I'd read that article in [major US punk zine] *Maximum Rocknroll* about like, 'Some rock stars are already this fucked …' – there was a guy with a gun in his mouth – which was written by Steve Albini. I have that article actually, that magazine. I didn't want to get into heaps of debt and then just have that hanging over us. So we kind of all decided *No*, and have never regretted it for a second. Although I have those moments of like the sliding doors, like *what would happen if we did?* Would we be as big as You Am I or Something for Kate? I don't think it would have happened to us because of who we are. But I just think that it might have caused problems that we didn't need, we already had enough. I don't regret it.

Joe Woolley: When you talk to Tumbleweed and you talk to Magic Dirt and you talk to Spiderbait, these guys were lucky to get a first record out on a major label. Every one of them will say: we fucking nearly broke up, it was that much pressure we couldn't handle it, we didn't know how to do it. I think that Screamfeeder, by virtue of having put at least two records out on Survival, and having got Triple J airplay and been touring and supporting Pavement and others … They looked at it and went, we have a certain level of control. We're quite independent in how we do things. We're getting along just fine. And our friends in these bands are telling us how horrible and awful it is.

Kellie: We were a day away from supposedly leaving to go tour America through [US label] Taang! Records. Taang! put out *Burn Out Your Name* and it was on vinyl and it was really exciting. They put out The Lemonheads and stuff like that. And Joe [Segreto], our manager [in the 1990s, not to be confused with current manager Joe Woolley] was dealing with … his name was Curtis and he just kind of dropped off the communication and we were ready to go, and then the tickets never came through, the money never came through and we were just like, *What do we do?* We'd played this big going away show and it was a fundraising gig now we're not going. It was really embarrassing. And it was also really devastating. And so we just went, *all right, well, we'll just keep going*, which is what we've always done when everything goes to shit, we just go, *well, let's just keep going*.

Tim: It's screamingly obvious that 'Wrote You Off' should have been a single: it's mega-catchy, it's melodic, it's uptempo, all the things. But the mood of the day, musically, was really about heaviness. Really that sort of hangover of the grunge thing.[15]

Kellie: We weren't thinking, we were just living. I didn't have any money, I was just living in clothes that I bought at op-shops or someone gave me, or like a band t-shirt from the band we played with the night before. I really loved just getting in a van and just going. *Bye, seeya later,* and we would just be gone. No one knew where we were unless they had our itinerary. I didn't have a partner or anything back then, so I was just disappearing. Maybe I'd get some change together and call my parents while I was away. Say oh, *I'm in Geelong,* or *I'm in Adelaide, I'm in Perth at the moment.* I loved sitting in a car and hurtling down the highway, listening to really loud music. And we only had to get to a gig. There was no real pressure on us, we weren't over-connected to everything like we are now with phones and computers. Sure we had to do a lot of work getting gigs and stuff, but when you're doing that driving, you're really free, and I really loved that time.[16]

Fill Yourself With Music (1995)

Tim: *Fill Yourself With Music* [1995] went off the edge of the cliff and we were like, *Oh fuck! What do we do?* It was so different. And rather than trying to build on what we had with *Burn Out Your Name,* we changed direction without really putting any thought into it. The songs were really different, like really weird.

Kellie: It's usually the difficult second record, but *Fill Yourself With Music* was our difficult third record.

Tim: It was December '94. We caught a bus down to Sydney to record at Paradise Studios, in Kings Cross. I didn't own a guitar at the time. I used to smash my guitars. I borrowed some guitars off Wayne [Connolly, producer], so I just used borrowed gear for the whole thing. We went in way less organised than we would have for our previous albums. It was done really on the fly, really *whatever happens happens.*

Kellie: We had been listening to a lot of stuff like The Flaming Lips, Guided By Voices, stuff that wasn't hi-fi. A lot of Sebadoh, as well. We'd also toured with Pavement by then. They were another huge influence.

Tim: We had Heinz from [Brisbane band] Not From There hanging around quite a bit. He recorded guitar on two songs.

Kellie: Alison from Smudge popped in. Jeremy from [magazine] *Hot Metal* came in for a visit. There was a lot going on in Sydney. You Am I played a gig that we all went to. We had dinner with Magic Dirt. The Fur girls popped in. It was a crazy time.

Tim: Tony and Kellie were having issues and it was a little stiff and a little hard to get along within the band.

Kellie: Tony used to throw things at me. We'd have screaming matches on the street. He hated me. I was drinking a lot, so I would fuck up at gigs. Before we went on this tour, Tony had said to Tim: *It's her or me.* Tim was like, *I don't want to make a choice*, he would do anything to avoid conflict. One night we played at this big festival in Sydney, and I had messed up. Afterwards, I sat down and started spilling out all the stuff that had happened, and it's really bad. Tony was there and he walked out, and all these other people were there too, like Kram [from Spiderbait] was there. It was a really bad way to do it, but I had no control over it. The next morning Tony flew home. Tim and I drove home on our own. We barely talked.

Andrew Stafford (*Rolling Stone*, July 1995): In separate interviews, both Blades and Lloyd admitted to tensions within the band. 'By the time this album comes out', said Lloyd, 'there will have been changes. Something has to give. But I can't say more than that'. Days before this issue of *Rolling Stone* went to press, Steward phoned. Blades was out of the band.

Kellie: Tim sent Tony a fax that everybody in the house saw. It was awful.

3 Side A

Writing *Kitten Licks*

By the middle of the 1990s, Screamfeeder had a distinct reputation – at least in the alternative national imaginary of community radio, zines, street press and pub gigs. They were heavy rockers with songwriting depth; critical darlings with live power; Brisbane underground overlords and touring ambassadors; and hard-working best-kept-secrets, already trailed by a should-have-been narrative. (Did you hear they were stood up by their US label just days before the flight? Why aren't they as big as Tumbleweed?) But their fourth album, Kitten Licks, captures the moment when the rest of the picture clicked into place. The classic songs, the classic sound, the classic lineup. As any student of rock or sociology will tell you, groups of three are as powerful as they are fragile, and changing one member can have a dramatic effect. For Screamfeeder, changing drummers sparked a chain reaction, touching everything from songwriting to singing. In many ways, the story of Kitten Licks is the story of Dean Shwereb joining the band.

Enter Dean

Tim: We saw Dean play in Hateman.[1] You couldn't take your eyes off him 'cause he looked amazing, sitting right up, chest out. He's playing these super slow songs and he was the master of them, he was fucking *insane*. We were like, *We gotta get that guy*. And we did.

Dean: They heard that Hateman broke up and I think they called the same day. I said, *I suppose I'll give it a go*, you know.

Kellie: I don't remember the first time we played together, but I know that we all went, *Wow, this is amazing!* And he was super nice. He brought his kit and he had all these brand new 'Girls Can Do Anything' stickers on it.

Tim: I think we were practising on Ann Street in the city, above the second-hand record shop. The first song he played might have been 'Lost in the Snow' [from *Fill Yourself With Music*]? Three bars in Kel and I were like, *Yep. That's fine* to each other. He gets to the end of the first song and it's like, *Yeah, you're in the band, you're fucking amazing!*

Dean: They'd just put out *Fill Yourself With Music* and they were going on a tour. I'm a quick learner and I was always into their stuff. I remember being in Hateman and I was listening to [English band] Swervedriver's *Mezcal Head* when it came out, but I was kind of hiding it, you know, because I didn't want the guys to know that I was listening to it. I was kind of always into indie-rock, just good guitar music.

Tim: He's so confident and upright. His style's so snappy, you can hear every little hit. And he's got flair and he knows how to use it. He's one of those drummers that's just got the magic ingredient.

Kellie: Tony [Blades, outgoing drummer] was very, I call it meat and potatoes, like Dave Grohl. Not that that's bad. Dean is like a spicy meatball, with kind of weird veggies in there. Just incredibly creative on the drums, like no one I know. He would play and he would just do rolls, and you never expected him to land it. But he did, and it was like *what?*

Dean: I was always trying to come up with good drum parts, just for myself. I always used to get stoned and try to come up with bent shit. I could always make a chorus come out and I've got a good song arrangement sensibility. It may not be the most technical Virgil Donati shit you'll ever hear – nothing wrong with Virgil Donati, Jesus Christ he could play – but I could make a song sound pretty good, y'know?

Damien Hughes (fan): I remember when they told me they had a new drummer. I met Dean for the first time and I thought he was a clown, in a good way. He was so funny! He was a crack up, man. I was in hysterics. When Dean had just joined the band, we were sitting in Adelaide in the hotel room and out of the blue he says, *Hey man, do you know where I can get cool clothes like what The Jam wear?* And I said, *Oh I dunno man, Mods R Us?* He goes, *Where's that?* All of us fucking lost it except for Dean! He thought it was a real place. So Screamfeeder started putting *Presented by Mods R Us* on their posters.

Kellie: When someone's two or three years younger than you, and you're in your mid-twenties and they're in their early twenties, it's like they're so young. He felt like a teenager, and he was so polite and always very on edge, trying to make sure he was doing the right thing.

Damien Hughes: He was kind of like the young dude that was just so happy to be in this position. And he was an amazing drummer. He was perfect for that band, like he got what they were about. I think it not only changed the dynamic of the band but I think maybe he helped change their sound. I remember the first time I heard 'Bridge Over Nothing', in Adelaide at the *Crown & Anchor Hotel*, and I just remember watching Dean's arms go everywhere because it's basically a drum roll through the whole song. I was amazed at his stamina to keep it up. Like how the fuck do you do that?

Writing *Kitten Licks*

Tim: I was living in St James Street in [inner Brisbane suburb] Petrie Terrace with my then-partner and my baby. I'd sit on the bed and write when everyone was asleep. Then we moved to [western Brisbane suburb] Bardon. I think my own writing was only probably a quarter of the whole picture, because most of the songs we threw together from an idea in the practice room, and then went home and wrote the words or finished the tune.

Kellie: There were only a few songs that were written beforehand, and everything else was written in the practice room. I'm pretty sure it was every day for two hours. We would practise and write.

Dean: It was pretty productive. We weren't mucking around. We were all pretty excited I guess. I was obviously young: no kid, no job, no family. You'd just play and go in there as much as you can. And you've got a lot of energy. I think I'd just turned twenty-one, so I could play all night, every night, and every day, probably. No biggie.

Tim: Behind the music shops on Barrie Parade in the Valley, there was a little basement room that four or five bands practised in. It was rammed full of gear and we went in before other bands came in to rehearse. We'd go in about six at night, come out about eight, and just bash stuff out, maybe three or four times a week. The three of us just had this thing, we could walk in and someone would go, *Oh, you start something*, and half an hour later there were the bones of a song. We'd go, *Yeah, that's great*, and then we'd do another one and head home.

Kellie: We'd come up with something, but we didn't have phones so we couldn't record them. Whoever stood up to the mic to sing on a riff, took that song [as lead vocalist].

Tim: It's crazy, we didn't have phones or any way of recording it, so we'd go home and remember it. Like, *Yeah, it goes like this*. And we'd be like, *Yeah, sure, it goes like that*. Like who could fucking remember it?

Kellie: I was really depressed [in that period] and then when Dean joined it was like a brand new chapter. The whole thing just felt wiped clean and brand new. There was heaps of freedom in the band room, and it was fun being in this environment where I was liberated to be able to do my songs, to contribute. And because I'd already worked so hard with Tim on previous records doing bass lines and that, we had this really great musical connection. We liked all the same stuff.

And he understood my need for quirky, weird things. I was always like, *Let's do something just kind of weird here.* We kind of fed into each other's creativity and we created a language as the three of us. We worked out how to talk drums to Dean, because you always have a drum language, and it opened everything up.

Tim: I think it was just so relaxed and easy in the room. Kel's big hurdle before was having Tony there 'cause he was quite critical and, not like it was a boy's club band, but he wasn't that open to Kellie singing. So she felt free enough to do it like no one was going to judge her. And we were always throwing ideas around. If you did something shit, it didn't matter and you weren't embarrassed 'cause everyone's playing stuff that's shit for a while, and then it would start coming together. And then once Kellie did sing, it was all on. We were like, every song, *We should both definitely sing on this song.*

Kellie: It was exciting to be able to sing together. We loved The Pixies, and there weren't a lot of bands doing that stuff. It wasn't so much about harmonising, it was about the dual vocal. It just became this thing that we really like to do. We could definitely sense that something was going on. It wasn't like we weren't thinking about other people liking it. We were liking it. And that's the thing, whenever we write music, it's not really thinking about other people. It's about whether we want to play it and whether we like it, and what do we like about it?

Tim: It's not just harmonies, it's trading. I think we're bad at harmonies 'cause none of us are pitch perfect Doing in-between stuff's way, way better. You can get away with more.

Kellie: I guess *Burn Out Your Name* was like heavy and dirgey and riffy. That said, I think that Tim definitely was more attuned to pop songs, and I was more the other way. But, thing is, I only write pop songs. I find it really hard to not write pop songs. Although they're never happy pop songs, they might sound happy, but have really down lyrics.

Tim: I always went for the punk stuff which had chords that had a melody going over them. Even in bands like Crass or Dead Kennedys, the more melodic songs were the ones I would come to. And then I got to Hüsker Dü, job done!

Damien Hughes: *Kitten Licks* is where I discovered their hidden secret, which is that they do everything in threes. They don't do everything in fours. Everything's in threes. And when I confronted Tim about that he goes, *Ah, you've found us out. We stole that off Hüsker Dü.* If you listen to the way they do chord progressions, everything cuts short.

Kellie: It keeps us on our toes. It's not to bamboozle other people, but we're just not happy with the song being just easy. It's kind of gotta have a little something in there.

Side A

'Static'

Tim: The little false intro is the old demo version of 'Static', where I think we might have played it down-tuned a step. Then the normal version kicks in. And the snare is fucking unbelievable! It's got this beautiful woody ring to it. I love it, it's my favourite snare sound ever. It's beautiful.

Paul McKercher (*Kitten Licks* producer): I love the intro to 'Static'. It sounds to me as though it's a little bit orchestral even, with the snare roll and then when it reappears later in the song, the guitar part is harmonised too. It's a fantastic piece of writing I reckon.

Tim: I used to get a lot of handmade zines. People would send them in the mail, it was awesome. There's one from America called *Dreamwhip,* with this story which is basically the lyrics of 'Static'. I stole it and moved the story around and put it into the song. And then I told the guy and he's like, *Thanks for asking.* I was like, *Oh sorry!* I think he was into it, but he would have appreciated being asked, which is fair enough. I wrote that one at St James Street at Petrie Terrace. It came together quickly: had the zine in front of me, just wrote it down and made it work, gave it to the band and it's exactly how I wrote it. I went back to this guitar tuning that we'd used a lot on *Burn Out Your Name.* The first three songs of *Kitten Licks* are in the same tuning [EADAAE]. Even though I love to use different tunings, 'cause they give a different voice, all the chords are mega-simple, straightforward chords. All the changes are just where you expect them to go, there's nothing fancy or clever.

Kellie: It's a big pop song. It definitely had a single quality about it, 'cause it was poppy and sing-alongy and it was really fun to play and jump up and down. I remember practising it a lot, and it was one of those songs where I always, always make the same mistake in it. I still probably make it.

'Bridge Over Nothing'

Kellie: So one of the things about Dean, he'd always say random things.

Tim: We're doing this photo session near the Kangaroo Point Cliffs and there's a little garden at the bottom. We're walking along and there's this weird little wooden bridge with nothing under it. And Dean's like, *That's a bridge over nothing.* I was like, thanks buddy. I think I wrote it at home. I showed Dean how the chords would feel and he just did that shit and we were like, [laughing] *Holy fuck this is amazing!* And perhaps we suggested, *Let's straighten it up in the chorus 'cause you're killing yourself here.*

Dean: I remember listening to Swervedriver's *Ejector Seat Reservation*. There was a song on it, 'I Am Superman'. I think I wanted 'Bridge Over Nothing' to be something like that.

Kellie: There's some footage of Dean playing the drums at the ABC, and he's just playing it so fast! And at the end of it I'm sitting there and I'm just like, *This guy! We did the right thing with this guy.*

'Dart'

Kellie: 'Dart' was probably the first time we ever collaborated fully. Tim came up with the riff and we came up with the structure. I stepped up to the mic and sang the chorus, but Tim was doing the verses. I wrote the lyrics. We all came up with the arrangement and we went over and over and over and over it, because it's got that weird beginning. The first time we nailed that beginning and the whole song, I was like, *Oh my God, this song is something else.* We knew we'd written something really amazing.

Dean: I think 'Dart' is the only one I kind of vaguely remember being in the practice room and playing. I remember that weird change in it at the start, like a weird timing or a hiccup.

Tim: We sweated over the two little turnaround points forever. I could hear it in my mind, but every time I went to try and explain what I was hearing, I couldn't really translate it and it just ended up how it is. It's so tight and it doesn't have any points where there's a bit of slack time, where you can take a breath. We wrestled it into shape in the practice room, took probably a couple of weeks and I think Kellie wrote all the lyrics.

Kellie: It's not about anything in particular, but each bit is about something. Tim didn't know this for a very long time, but the first part's about my period. It's about being premenstrual: *I'm neat in cycles.* I wanted to put the word *cram* in there 'cause of Kram from Spiderbait, I loved the name Kram! So many people thought it was about heroin, or about drugs. But yeah, Tim didn't know that it was kind of like a journal entry about being a girl.

Tim: We were reading a lot of Martin Amis books at the time. We were reading *London Fields* and they always call a cigarette a 'dart', so that's where the title comes from. I can't remember how we came up with the chorus, the interlocking thing, but the moment we did we were like, *Oh fuck that's good. This is cool!* It might have been really the first big one where we did the dual vocals. That was opening the door.

'Bruises'

Tim: I was trying to mimic Regurgitator, in their very smart, quick songwriting. Quickly get to the chorus, quickly get out again, very fast. I guess my default is to fall towards lyrics about distress or heartbreak or whatever, like a lot of songwriters. Honestly with probably 50 per cent of my songs I'll start playing and my mouth will open, and something will come out and by the time I've got two lines I'm like, *OK, I'm on track.* I'm really quite strict with myself about phrasing the syllables. I was bored with normal tuning, bored with playing C and G chords. I knew bands like Swervedriver and Sonic Youth were using different tunings. The 'Bruises' tuning is actually one that Tim Rogers showed me. He used that one a lot on early You Am I stuff. You drop the A string to G. It's a Rolling Stones tuning. I used it for 'Explode Your Friends', 'Bruises', 'Dead to the World', and 'Broken Ladder'. You can add on notes you wouldn't be able to otherwise. It's cheeky, you know.

Kellie: I sing the *I know, I know* bits. And Tim wanted me to sing it in a bit of a sexy way, like a bit more sort of breathy. But I was like, [shouting] *I know, I know!* I got what he meant years later. Like, *Oh, I should sing it like that, a bit sassy.* I was just doing the wrong kind of sass. I learned the right sass years later. The ending, I always think it's like a Damned song, 'New Rose'. That's always heaps of fun. One of the things we like to do is have a thing that happens once, and it's something that you might want more and more, but it's always better to leave people hanging and wanting more of it.

Paul McKercher: Often fast tempo stuff feels like it's a car chase or as though you're running late for the bus, and you're getting a bit tangled up. But they really nailed the fast tempos with a lot of confidence. I thought it sounded like that headfirst plunge towards the future that youth has, where it's fast and there's no shits given and you just want to get to the end of whatever the current preoccupation is. I always loved that about fast tempo stuff that sounded pacey but controlled. 'Bruises' was one of them.

'Explode Your Friends'

Tim: I think we were listening to [New York band] Girls Against Boys, and they had this real slow groove thing going. That was our influence on this and 'Dead to the World'. A bit more restrained, heavier tempo. The chorus was the first time we'd ever done anything like that: just sing, *Come on, oh come on, oh come on,* over and over. Maybe that's a bit like Girls Against Boys as well, cool and groovy. Lyric-wise, I don't know, It's random. It happened. My partner at the time, Micki, did the purring on there. She was very good at purring.

Kellie: That's a definite Tim song, 'cause I'm like: what do you mean *explode your friends*?

Tim: Can't remember what it's really about anymore, or rather where the inspiration came from. Kinda about having days where even your friends seem alien to you. Dean once said that if he dies he'd want to come back as an alien. That might have given me the idea, but I couldn't actually fit it into the song.[2]

Kellie: But I love playing that song. It's so much fun to play and it was actually really hard to learn as well, cause it does that three thing. I'm strumming a lot of stuff and that's my favourite thing to do on the bass. I just wanted to strum high notes. Playing chords on the bass was me trying to be Robert Smith, it was just The Cure. Learning 'A Forest' and 'Primary' and going, *This is the best way to play the bass.* And because we were a three piece it fills out the sound. It's much heavier, and looks really cool. It's a lot of fun and it changes everything. No one taught me that, I had to learn that myself. And then playing all that noisy stuff, I could scratch my pick, and get weird.

Tim: It's so funny because that portion of the song where it loosens off is … literally in about the last five years, I've learned how to play it correctly and put things in the right place so that the chords are right. And on the record they're wrong, like minor where there should be major and weird notes that should not be there.

'Down the Drinker'

Kellie: I wrote that song in about as much time as it takes to play it. It was like, *pew, bam, the song is born!* I remember writing it at my desk at Warmington Street in Paddington. I just sat there and I wrote the whole thing, like even the little [sings high two-note guitar part]. I was ripping off Magic Dirt.

Tim: Kel's song about short people. She always announces it with, *This song's for all the short girls in the room.* [3]

Kellie: I still have the lyrics. I wrote them all out right at that moment. It's like I inhabited another person for that period of time. It's about a little kid who is kind of never enough, and feels like their family needs them to win and they don't care about it. And it's so weird, it doesn't reflect me, 'cause I was never in a family like that. But it's like I became a little character and I wrote this song for that little character, and that's the end of the story. I've never done that again or before.

Tim: I think the only input I had was this chord change. The second one goes to C-sharp or something instead of the E, that's the only input I had. The song structure was a piece of piss to put together. The funny thing about it is that we didn't record on a click, so all the stops are a little loose.

4 Side B

Recording *Kitten Licks*

Sonically, Kitten Licks *sits in a sweet spot. To fans of Screamfeeder's previous work, it shines with a new clarity. To fresh ears, it is excitingly raw, 'a burning gem' (Grimson, 1996). Upon release,* Kitten Licks *captured the aural excitement of a new wave of distinctively Australian and youthful rock. Yet decades later, it is surprisingly undated and cosmopolitan. The album is musically detailed, by the standards of a three-piece rock band playing three-minute pop songs: odd numbers of bars, one-off fills, hairpin turns, stops and starts. But the presentation is lean, muscular and intense, registering above all as* live. *To a degree, these aesthetic qualities are the result of material realities.*

For Screamfeeder in 1996, the recording money fronted by their independent label was a step up; by wider industry standards it was a shoestring. But working tight and fast is exactly what this band did. Less than a year on from their last album release, Screamfeeder had recruited a new drummer, written a swag of songs (most of them in a three-month burst from February to April), completed demo recordings (with Jeff Lovejoy at Red Zeds Studios in Brisbane) and booked into Rockinghorse Studios, inland and uphill from the coastal town of Byron Bay in northern New South Wales, for two weeks in May. In hindsight, this was also a threshold moment for their Sydney-based producer Paul McKercher, and for Australian music. With a CV including the cult and cutting-edge (The Apartments, Clouds, The Cruel Sea, Hoodoo

Gurus, Tumbleweed), Paul had recently recorded You Am I's Hourly, Daily *(along with Wayne Connolly who recorded* Fill Yourself With Music). *That You Am I album, when released later in the year after ongoing inter-label negotiations, would debut at #1 and reap a clutch of ARIA (Australian Recording Industry Association) awards for the band and producers, including both* Album of the Year *and* Independent Release of the Year, *marking a peak in the mainstream embrace of local alternative rock – along with the multi-million dollar purchase of their label, rooArt, by BMG Australia. Given their earlier brush with the label, we might expect this news to catch Screamfeeder's attention. But in May, winding their way up muddy roads in the north-east New South Wales hinterland, the rest of the world felt far away.*

Rockinghorse Studios

Kellie's Diary: Day 1 – Wed 1 May 1996

Arriving at the studio amidst torrential rains. The car was so packed it was amazing that we could fit in it at all. Through the city [leaving Brisbane] I was driving and couldn't see a thing. People were honking at us as we changed lanes. It turned dark and started raining early and we only had one headlight working, it was only if the lights were on full beam that both worked.

We got to the studio ok and Divvy, the house engineer drove us out to the house which is past Federal.[1] It's a fantastic place that is all wood and glass with a wood burner and a verandah that goes all the way around the house. The bathroom is all white tiles with huge windows and a glass shower so you feel like you're showering in the yard. The yard is unreal, lots of fruit trees and it's all so green.

It's now been raining since we've been here continuously without end, where is all this water coming from?

Paul [McKercher, producer] was supposed to arrive at 10 the first night. By midnight we had gone to bed and I was getting worried about him. Thinking what do we do if he's had an accident and we're without a producer?

The next day he still wasn't here. So I called the studio. Paul was there but only just. He'd driven from Sydney in his Valiant and it had taken him 15 hours. He'd arrived at the studio and Divvy gave him directions to get to the house. He almost got here, but got bogged before he made it. He got out and even walked to the house, but went back to his car and tried to sleep. No use. He walked for an hour and a half back to the studio where he slept. He arrived here finally at the house and we made pancakes and coffee.

It took us 3 or 4 hours to get stuff set up and by 5pm we attempted our first takes.

The studio and its surrounds are unreal. Looking out the window it's lush bushland and rolling hills.

It wasn't until after dinner we relaxed and got some good takes. Dean was getting a bit stressed out about his playing and so did I for a while. But we left feeling pretty happy.

Day 2 – 2 May 1996

No let-up in the rain. I'm scared we are going to get bogged.

Tim: I think [our label] Shock just said, *This is the budget.* They must have chosen Paul because we didn't know him, though we definitely knew the name. They probably chose the studio because they were in charge of the money, or maybe Paul suggested the studio.

Paul: Some records that were well-budgeted by major record companies would have six figure budgets attached to them. I think the budget on this one was about $20,000, so it was really bare bones.

Kellie: Shock had the money and they believed in us, and I guess Joe [Segreto, band manager] was negotiating and we were a hard-working touring band, so it kind of made sense, we just happened to have all the right things happening at the right time.

Paul: I was aware of them through *Burn Out Your Name*, which was getting some airplay on Triple J, where I worked until 1993, '94. The word on the street was that they were a very strong band and they played really well, they wrote really well, they gave good live performances. Amongst my muso friends, Screamfeeder were a band to watch out for.

Kellie: Rockinghorse was a well-known studio. For us, it was big.

Paul: I made a lot of records in that studio and people loved going there. Byron Bay was a twenty-five-minute drive down the hill and it was much more rural back then. It wasn't as much of a tourist destination. It was kind of a cool place to go and hang and let off a bit of steam, so it wasn't as though we were stuck in the bush. Cheap drugs were plentiful and easily available, and that caused quite a bit of distraction for some of the artists that I've worked with. But Screamfeeder worked very hard and they knew that we had a limited amount of time to get it done.

Kellie: We didn't really go to Byron at all, 'cause like it was like ten-hour days in the studio. It wasn't a holiday. It was work. We would work whenever Paul was ready, until whenever he was done.

Dean: We were in the hinterland, it was just like you were in the country. It's not like we ended up in town or anything. I do remember getting in trouble for eating the food a bit too much.

Kellie: It was a really fun session. We would all drive together in the car to the studio and work all day. We'd eat well 'cause we were cooking, we had to shop and have all our own food there. We'd go back and this house we were staying at was absolutely beautiful. There were people that would come and stay like my partner Stephen, and Paul and his partner and baby. It was high stakes, a bit of high pressure, but it was fun. I really enjoy recording. Some people hate it but I just love it.

Dean: The accommodation was a little drive away. You'd drive down to the studio, it's just like this little house. The drum room downstairs and then next floor up, a little walk-up, was the studio room, the mixing desk. It was just one big room downstairs, looking out to the bush or the country. I just remember it was constantly raining.

Tim (on *Recovery*, 1997): When we were recording our new album, at the studio there was a ping pong table. It was always raining so we couldn't go outside and do much. And so every half an hour or so, whenever we felt the tension rising, we'd go outside and have a game of ping pong. And it was really great, and ever since then we've been hooked on ping pong.

Gear

Dean: I had a real cheap Pearl Export kit, this cheap, nasty kit I bought when I was a kid. Did the job I guess. But I think I possibly did have my Dad's Ludwig snare, and a wooden Yamaha snare. I had that because I was getting into Dinosaur Jr's snare sound, and I was like, *That sounds like it's wood*, but I don't know whether it was or not. I think it was done on the Yamaha snare.

Kellie: I believe that I used what was there, and it would have been like an Ampeg SVT 1, a big, enormous, analogue bass amplifier. It would have been that for sure.

Figure 1 *The recording console at Rockinghorse Studios. Photo by Stephen Booth.*

Tim: I think at the time I had a Marshall amplifier, you know the heads with the four inputs, where you can cross one over with a patch lead? And my MXR Distortion+ [pedal]. That was the set-up. Same set-up for every song. That was the method back then. *Kitten Licks* was the first album I had Tele Deluxe [Fender Telecaster Deluxe guitar]. I got it because Heinz from [fellow Brisbane outfit] Not From There was playing one. I loved it and I was like, *Dude, if you ever see another of those guitars, get it for me.* And he was on the coast one day, and he called me up and said, *I found one of those guitars, thirteen-hundred bucks.* I was like, *Get it.* The guitar sound on the album is very – it sounds like that guitar, it's got this very mid-rangey kind of thing going on. Darek [Mudge] is like, *You can never sell that guitar, it's the Screamfeeder sound.* 'Cause I kind of get sick of it every so often, he's like, *No!*[2]

Paul: The album was committed to a beautiful sounding tape machine through some wonderful sounding Neve outboard, a lot of Pultecs, a lot of Ureis. Classic rock and roll equipment. Stuff that is still highly valued today was in that control room. The desk was some sort of an entry-level Tascam but it did the job and things sounded good.

Studio Time

Paul: We made a very solid sounding record in fourteen days, recorded and mixed, which was a record time for that period. Generally to track a record might have been from three weeks to six weeks. I was used to mixing a song a day, so to mix a record would take two weeks.

Tim: It was a super quick recording session. Paul didn't fuck around trying to spend days getting good sounds. We just mic'd everything up and went for it. Paul was right on board with the vibe, like he got it, he liked the songs. I assume he'd heard the demos. We didn't have any pre-production sessions with him or anything like that.

Paul: They all had very strong sounds that they'd been working up for some time. This was a hard working band, that had been together for a number of years already, so they were pretty well dialled in. From an engineering point of view it was as good as it gets. I thought the acoustics of the rooms were beautiful, the drums especially, and Dean – Dean the Machine as we called him – he played fantastically on that record. He played with great fire, and he and Kellie locked right in. If you've got good drums it's sort of 75 per cent of your record. If you've got a drummer that's laying things down clearly and confidently, it just improves everybody else's performance. And Dean is fantastic on that record.

Dean: No wonder I ate all the food, I was banging out drum take after drum take for like two days. I was twenty-one. No wonder I was hungry.

Paul: When you're on a fourteen-day schedule, the band needs to perform. Everyone needs to know their parts and to perform strongly and for the engineer to do their job well. And listening to the record, I can't hear a single uncertain or unconfident note or bar. That's impressive, particularly because the technology at the time didn't really allow you to fix up average performances. Tape editing takes time and costs money. As the record progressed, you'd have less and less usable tape. You had to decide, *Can we get a better take of this?* Actually it's good pressure, because it puts more pressure on the band to perform well.

Tim: Dean was obviously on fire, so we didn't have too many takes. Probably did like two takes at the most of each song, and a quick couple of guitar and bass overdubs. Our approach is super simple, there's usually just stereo guitar tracks, occasionally, maybe, a bit of extra guitar, but not much.

Paul: I think there is one sound on the whole record that you wouldn't hear the band be able to make themselves, and that's a backward cymbal in 'Pigtails on a Rock'. And that is the only sound on the record that isn't a naturally occurring sound as generated by the band.

Dean: There's a thing that happens in 'Bridge Over Nothing', it sounds like a backward cymbal. It's actually a gong. It's called a wind gong, and you keep hitting it and it builds up and then you stick it between your legs and it makes that sound. It fluctuates in the middle and that fucking killed me. It's nothing, it goes for like a split second. But it just kills me. It just makes me want to fucking kick shit.

Paul: I was a huge fan of pretty much anything Steve Albini did, his work on Nirvana's third album [*In Utero*] and with the Pixies. I think we were all fans of that. His production philosophy was to take the producer out of the picture pretty much, a very documentarian approach where you capture the energy that's in the room at the time. And I think that was probably the only option I had, actually. On a two week record there was no time to be doing lots of overdubs. I think the vocal overdubs all happened right at the end, so that really puts a lot of pressure on all bands as that window gets smaller and smaller, to get on the mic and perform really well.

Kellie: You had to perform. You had to be on it. And there wasn't a lot of room to move. When I was doing my vocals, Paul suggested that brandy was really good to warm up your throat. So I got really drunk on brandy and I had to redo all my vocals the next day.

Kellie's Diary: Day 6 – Monday 6 May 1996

I'm doing my vocals. Drinking brandy to let it flow.
Getting pretty drunk.
There is always a bit of opposing egos happening – Tim and I going head to head for a while. It's like he's opposing my creative vision especially on my songs.
I've never bought 2 packets of cigarettes at once before.

Figure 2 *Kellie Lloyd and guest cellist Luke O'Sullivan practise outside the band's accommodation before recording. Photo by Stephen Booth.*

Today I did.
My ears are really ringing.
My vocals are going ok.
I think.
Cigarette time.

Paul: They rose to the occasion. Every word is delivered with believability and intention and purpose, and it's completely convincing.

Kellie: It rained the entire time. And the only time it stopped was the last day, and that was when Luke [O'Sullivan] came to do cello. He arrived early in the morning and I got up and we sat outside in the sun and practised the song. Everyone woke up in the house and came out and it was like this magical blue-sky day. I mean there's nothing like cello. And you know, it's in the bush, there was no one, no neighbours or anything, and it was just magical.

Mixing, Mastering, Sequencing

Tim: When we got to the mixing, we'd do three or four songs a day. Paul would set it up, go, *How is it?* And we'd go, *That's good, why don't you do this, that or the other?* And then it would be all-hands-on-deck, three of us on the desk, putting reverbs on or fading. It's really fun actually, it's hilarious fun doing that. A bit of that and we'd have it in the bag.

Paul: It all sounds very natural. There's no production artifice whatsoever. It's very documentary, I just wanted to present what I had on tape. I was a formally trained recording engineer, so I understood concepts of information capture; that the movement of the air molecules as excited by the musicians and the way that they play is almost infinitely complex, and that you're only really capturing a bit of a slice of it. It's an audio photograph, if you like, but the clarity of that audio photograph is incredibly important, because woven into that complexity is the emotional intention of the player. And so if you can get that in the audio photographs that you take, and have that emotional intention come out the speakers at the other end of the process once it's been mixed and mastered and people get to listen to it, then the job is achieved. And you've done justice to the music and to the musician who's playing it.

Kellie: It would have been Tim over his shoulder telling him to put up the guitars and me over his shoulder saying, *Put up the bass.*

Tim: I went to Germany with my partner and kid immediately after recording, before mastering. I was listening back to the tape and when you've just recorded, you get super precious like, *I fucked that, that, and that*, pointing to all these little flaws. I was ringing up the mastering dude going, *Can you get this on 'Explode Your Friends' and on the second dropout just cut like a millisecond out of it?* And everyone was like, *Dude, chill.* And I was like, *OK, I'm just gonna have to let it be what it is.* Nowadays I can't even hear it.

Kellie: It's always fun putting a track listing together. We would have really laboured over the order as we do with every album, so we would have had cassettes with different orders to listen to them. In the middle of the album there's a pivot, and it would have been made specifically to be: up front getting everybody in, like creating a mood and a really exciting sounding record; then it turns into a bit more of a thoughtful, interesting, unusual kind of record, and then ends with like the real epics. Which is kind of how most records we would put together would go.

Tim: The way the songs kind of overlap, that was just done on the fly as well. I don't like gaps on records. Mastering back then, we barely used any references, so we wouldn't put on an album we liked and go, *OK, we need to make it a little more mid-rangey* or whatever. You'd just go, *Yeah, that sounds good. Fine.* Next to the unmastered mix, the mastered mix is gonna sound better, and you'd go, *Yeah, sounds great.* Every time!

Dean: It sounds *huge*, Tim's guitars and that, you know? I just don't think he's got a better guitar sound on record since *Kitten Licks*.

Tim: It's probably my fave. It sounds so killer and Dean's just on fire. It's not a big guitar album, it's a drum and vocal album almost, and it's super exciting for that reason. I think it just captures that lucky moment we happened upon, the three of us, we just found ourselves in the space and time, and it was just lucky and fortuitous and amazing, serendipitous, all that stuff, you know? It was the time, the place, and we just captured it, and it was so lucky.

Side B

'Dead to the World'

Tim: 'Dead to the World' was taken from a Douglas Coupland book, *Shampoo Planet*. I don't know if it's dated now but his first six or eight are fucking amazing. Me and Kel both read them all.

Especially the last verse about the canaries and stuff, the book actually closes with this scene. Someone says *the world is alive*, and that's the last line of the whole book.

Kellie: He steals things from books and conversations. I love this song but I think the end lyric should be *the world is a lie*. I guess that's our personalities right there.

Tim: There were heaps of songs where we didn't know how to start, and we'd just say to Dean, *Can you do something?* And after one or two tries, he'd do something. 'Bruises', 'Dead to the World', 'End of the Wire', heaps of songs. We'd go *start it* and he'd come up with something awesome.

Kellie: That's my big Jesus Lizard moment. You listen to certain things and you just want to do those things. I wanted to play like slinky bass lines. And when the drums go *diddly-dit* and we stop and we start on the second note, that took forever. We just have to do those little things.

'Gravity'

Tim: 'Gravity' was me and Kel, line by line. A total practice room throw-together, just like *What should we do next? How about this?* If we'd gone in the next night we'd have a different song. The chords go together easily, it moves in an intuitive way. This is the only song where we chill out for a bit.

Kellie: I love the cute little bass line. It's backwards. That was one of the things I was playing around with and we would jam on, and we turned it into this thing.

Tim: The chorus is probably the least great part of it. A bit of a cheesy Nirvana rip-off, almost, which just doesn't really work too well.

Damien Hughes: I remember the first time I heard the chorus of that, and I looked out at the audience and everyone was just bopping along, like they were there right with them, because that chorus is so damn catchy.

Kellie: The lyrics were all out of my journal when I was high, on Valium, drinking wine. I was in [Sunshine Coast tourism destination] Noosa on a break, kind of getting away. I wrote all this stuff about the sea turning silver. It was about sensual things. I think that's when people thought that Tim and I were a couple, 'cause it's call and response and it does sound like … you know, all the tongues and stuff. Tim never said, *This is weird*, and I never thought it was weird. It just happened. 'I swallow pins' is about a serial killer, 'cause I used to read a lot about serial killers. Tim wrote the chorus, the gravity part. We shared this practice room with the Melniks or one of [Melniks drummer/ singer] Cass's bands, and we left the lyrics, it was typed up and printed. And because it says, 'I like the smoothness of cheese as it slides down' or whatever, Cass said to me, *I found these lyrics and it must be the other band's. I thought oh my God, who writes songs like that?* And I'm like, *It's me! it's my lyrics!* And I know, they're so weird!

'Ant (Demo)'

Tim: That would have been *Dean, can you start something? Kellie, can you put a bass line on it?* And then I'd just play some shit over it and it was just another totally five-minute practice room thing. We always liked to get a bit of shit going on, then straighten it up, then go back to the weird shit, then straighten it up. The big breakdown in the middle, Dean just did stuff like that, and me and Kel would stand there like, *That's great, it's in the song!*

Kellie: Again I just wanted to play like the Jesus Lizard. But it's really fast and it fucking hurts. I'm playing like all over this big rectangle, and I just get a cramp up my arm as soon as I start playing it, and I've got to sing through it as well. So I'm like (teeth gritted) *I will be good, I will be good"* while I'm grimacing and it kind of makes for a good vocal take.

Tim: The first verse is about me as a kid, in the class getting tied to my chair. That really happened. You could do shit back then to kids and parents didn't complain. When the teacher did it, I got up and ran around with a chair tied on my arse!

Kellie: At the end, where Dean does his little *dooga-dooga …dooga-dooga …* we worked on that for ages and we got to the point where, when we played it live, he would *really* slow it down. We're facing forward so we can't see him, 'cause we have to sing immediately. We just did it so many times that we know instinctively when he's gonna hit the thing.

Tim: The 'Ant' demo we recorded with Jeff Lovejoy at Red Zeds and it's like, that's all you need. The slowed-down drums bit was the tape running slow at the end of 'Dead to the World'.

Kellie: I love the piano. I worked that out on the piano at the studio where we did *Burn Out Your Name*. I'd just play it over and over and over. And 'Helen's Theme', that's my mum's name. We recorded it at the *Fill Yourself with Music* session, and it came out on this record. We've never played it live or anything. But Hüsker Dü always had the little piano interludes and this album doesn't have an acoustic song, which was a big thing in the 90s. Well, this is a bit of a nod to Hüsker Dü and it's for my mum. She doesn't know that, she's probably never listened to it. That's OK.

'End of the Wire'

Kellie: It's another thing from a book. He stole that idea from a book, I can't remember what book it was.

Tim: I feel that was stolen from Douglas Coupland as well, maybe *Shampoo Planet*, I got this loose story from and pushed it around into a song. Those early Douglas Coupland books are very sweet and naive and innocent. You can tell it was written in a really natural, fast-flowing way, and the way he tells stories, it makes you feel them. I wrote it and brought it to the band. I think I was trying to be a bit clever with the chords, as you can hear. It just gets by, it doesn't sound too clumsy.

Kellie: It's a really complicated pop song. Like, it's got all these fucking chords. *Stop it with the chords!* And all in different arrangements, one chorus is one way, the second chorus has got another added-on bit and they're all backwards. And I still get it wrong.

Darek Mudge: This was brought back into the set recently. We play it in a different key now. It's such a weird structure. If we haven't played it in a little while, one of us will stuff it. Except, Tim gets it every time, because he's a machine.

'Broken Ladder'

Tim: The title is from the Wim Wenders film *Until the End of the World*. We used to live on Heussler Terrace in Milton and I was like, *I've got nothing to do tonight, I'm gonna go to the movies on my own*. So I cycled over to St Lucia [riverside suburb that houses the University of Queensland with its Schonell Theatre cinema], had a joint and saw that film and I was like, *Holy fuck that's my favourite film ever!* I think Broken Ladder is the codename of one of the dudes in it. But the title was tacked on last. The song was written because there's a Liz Phair song called 'Shane' on *Whip Smart* and the last half of the song is this really boring, repeated line that goes forever – 'You've gotta have fear in your heart' – and it just goes between these two chords for minutes. You get hypnotised into it and it's really beautiful. I nicked it from there and wrote a song around it. It's all heartbreaky stuff. I wasn't heartbroken. It's just easy to write about that stuff. There's a line in it which is *bones can powder, blood can catch fire in my veins*. I stole that from somewhere, but I can't remember where. Almost all our songs are like fishing from here, there and everywhere, you know?

Kellie: I think some of the lyrics are stuff I'd said to Tim about Tony. Like, *Never call me worse things than you get called yourself/ listen to you never calm/never realise that words could do such harm*. And there's another thing like *bones can powder, blood can set fire in my veins/it won't compare to what i've carried in my brain*. So I remember having this conversation with Tim about how Tony would say off-handed, throw-away things that are just devastating to me, but I'll carry them around in my body forever and they just don't exist to him anymore. So Tim just distilled all this stuff into this song, which I don't even know if it's really about that or not for him. But he's just stolen stuff. He absorbs stuff and creates this amazing song out of things. I really love the lyrics on this, and I play big chords. I do the lead break at the end and that's so much fun. I'm all over the place on the bass on that one.

Tim: It got taken off the US version, ha! Not commercial enough for them (wankers).[3]

'Pigtails on a Rock'

Tim: Kellie threw it together in the practice room, doing harmonics.[4]

Kellie: I do it and then Tim does it and we have to count how many times we do it. It took forever to get it right. It's me trying to be like [American 'slowcore' band] Codeine or something, to bring in those elements of that very different music that I loved. It's very hard to do. It's one of my songs. It's very personal 'cause it's about, breaking up. Not necessarily about Tony but about being vulnerable, I suppose. 'Pigtails on a Rock' was an image of being a cute little girl who's just got no facial expression. It's a song about having to deal with being a person, I suppose. And we didn't play it very often, and I also couldn't listen to it. 'Cause it's like ugh, the vocal thing, but also because of what it is about.

Tim: It ended up super long because it has great grooves going on. And the sax thing and the cello came at the very last moment.

Kellie: We stole that off Swervedriver, 'Never Lose That Feeling'. It was like, *Let's do that!* And the song goes down in volume and then comes up again, so that's kind of our idea of a reprise, like you would see written on jazz records. *Let's do a reprise! What even is a reprise? Just fade it out and bring it back!*

Tim: This song is an example of where I was, like, *I gotta be on every song with the singing*, and I just put something in which really wasn't necessary. But you know how there's those two lines, 'Pigtails on a rock', and one of them is dry, then the reverb gets switched on for the second one? That was a mistake as we were running it out. Paul McKercher was like, *Oh fuck we haven't got the reverb on*, and put it on for the second line and it's fucking great. I love it. It's like, *Wow, this is a really exciting moment.* We didn't want to run it out again, so we just left it.

5 This Is It

Selling *Kitten Licks*

In The Sell-In *(2000), journalist Craig Mathieson outlines the adoption of 1990s Australian alternative music by mainstream industries and audiences, elevating some underground culture but also blurring once-important lines between independent and corporate activity. Within the decade, 1996 was a watershed year. In January of '96, the first Homebake festival was staged in a muddy field at Byron Bay, attracting a capacity crowd of 12,000 to an all-Australian bill topped by returning US conquerors silverchair, alongside recent Triple J Unearthed winners Grinspoon, and filled out by Magic Dirt, Powderfinger, Regurgitator, Spiderbait, Tumbleweed, You Am I (who cancelled due to injury) – and Screamfeeder. These acts and a handful of others became regulars on the growing national festival circuit for years to follow. In April that year, ABC television launched the music variety show* Recovery, *which beamed the same bands into the nation's lounge rooms every Saturday morning for the rest of the decade. And every one of the bands named above released music in 1996, including more than a few debuts and milestones.* Kitten Licks *is among them.*

On stage and screen, Australian bands of the mid-to-late 1990s appeared between and beside international stars, accruing a new form of home-grown pop celebrity with a national, 'all-ages' audience. Screamfeeder were never the most famous or commercially successful of this crop, nor did they visibly aspire to be. Yet in the wake of Kitten Licks, *they exemplified just how far a truly independent band – to use the material term pushed aside by the conveniently nebulous 'alternative' – could reach in this peculiar moment, which also happened to be the historical peak of the global record industry. As one of Brisbane's 'big four' bands, Screamfeeder staked a lasting place for their city alongside counterparts Powderfinger, Regurgitator and Custard. Yet the restlessly ambitious Screamfeeder was already looking further afield, including to the United States, where both the limitations of independence and the perils of incorporation were most apparent.*

Smoking Dog Press zine #2, 1996

SDP: *You've always had a great deal of respect in the press but only a moderate amount of success, unlike Tumbleweed, Spiderbait or Regurgitator. With this album there seems to be a buzz sort of generating around it – you've had rave reviews in every magazine, JJJ [Triple J] are flogging it and made it album of the week. Do you feel that this could be a breakthrough of sorts for you?*

Kellie: *Yes.*

Tim: *Well you're right in saying that we've always had really good reviews but never sold a lot of records, isn't that right Kell.*

Kellie: *Yes.*

Tim: *But it would be nice if this was a breakthrough for us and we could sell a lot more than 1500 copies throughout the whole country, and people come to shows … so it'd be nice, but we're not holding our breath, you know what I mean.*

Tim: Everything sort of coalesced, it was building up in '92, '93, '94, but that's when it all just went BOOM. It was super exciting and great.

Craig Mathieson (*Juice*, October 1996): 'I'm going to build a radio/With static from the stars,' sings Screamfeeder vocalist/guitarist Tim Steward on 'Static,' opening the Queensland trio's fourth album. It's a grand claim, but *Kitten Licks* lives up to it. As an album it has a remarkable drive, the result being a zealously melodic collection of pop/punk jewels that overtake 1995's *Fill Yourself With Music*. […] As we're awaiting new albums from silverchair, Magic Dirt and Spiderbait, Screamfeeder have pre-empted them with a memorable distillation of the magic that can still be found in guitar, bass, drums and voice. Make sure the prophecy hidden within 'Static' – 'The signal will get lost/In all the white noise floating by … ' – doesn't come true.

Mary Mihelakos (*Beat*, 14 August 1996): Had Screamfeeder come from Massachusetts rather than Townsville they would have been playing to and filling thousand plus capacity venues everywhere. But it has been a hard slog for Australia's hardest working band. […] Hopefully the public embrace of *Kitten Licks* will mean one less underrated and under appreciated band in this country. (9/10)

(*EG*, 16 August 1996): Never mind BritPop, could this be OzPop? Brisbane's Screamfeeder on this, their fourth album, have delivered a meaty, jangly, fast-driving collection of 12 songs that go quite some way towards defining a pop aesthetic which is both distinctive and unbeholden to overseas trends.

Tracey Grimson (*Rolling Stone*, September 1996): Queensland trio Screamfeeder are somewhat misunderstood in this country (not fitting comfortably into any pre-existing indie rock mould), yet they tend to be viewed with a degree of reverence. […] On *Kitten Licks*, Screamfeeder kick out an album that brims with slightly twisted power pop, with plenty of vocal interplay and the kind of hooks that evoke nothing less than a feverish grin. […] Screamfeeder are most capably beating their pop drum on this record and the result is a burning gem.

Andrew Stafford (*Time Off*, 9 September 1996): You've really got to credit Screamfeeder for coming this far. They've never achieved the profile of the likes of You Am I or Tumbleweed, but through sheer hard work and determination they're still here – and we are the better for it. And so are Screamfeeder. Their fourth album, *Kitten Licks* sees the band step out from the shadows of grunge into a rarefied, passionate pop form comparable only to the likes of Buffalo Tom. On that score alone, it's their best record. ****

Damien Hughes: When I heard *Kitten Licks* I was like, *This is it. This is how you are supposed to sound. This is the sound of Screamfeeder!* They really honed in on what their strengths were as a band. Kellie really shines on that record, not only as a songwriter but as a vocalist as well. The production is so perfect; the guitar tones are great, the drums sound great, the bass is phenomenal. And the playing is there.

Steve Bell (journalist): I remember buying the album and just being smitten by it. It was this crystallisation of everything that they'd been working towards. It just seemed like what you'd hope that they would make. Maybe Dean's drumming gave them a bit more space to explore the vocal interplay between Tim and Kellie, because that started being more prevalent and that's really part of their charm. I mean they both bring great stuff to the table, but when they do it together it's peak Screamfeeder.

Seja Vogel (musician): It's a collection of excellent riffs and hooks. 'Dart' made me fall in love with male/female call and response in songs.

Kate Cooper (musician): It's always been about the perfect songwriting for me. That and having a female and male vocalist. Hearing that when I was a kid for the first time was mind blowing. I could relate to it because there was a woman singing. Triple J only arrived on the Gold Coast [100 km south of Brisbane] in I want to say '95 or '96? Am I right? That period of time was so formative for me. The radio was awash with all this music that was blowing my mind. It was like how I imagine it was getting a colour TV. Prior to that, living on the coast the best we got was some gnarly commercial radio station playing top forty hits. I couldn't relate to any of it, so I just listened to my dad's records. To turn the radio on and hear this wild indie rock expanded my horizons. And my mind. It totally changed the course of my life.

Kate McGuire (musician): This record is just the epitome of cool sounding music. There isn't a thing about it I would change. I think my favourite thing about *Kitten Licks*, and

Screamfeeder in general is the dual vocals. They complement each other better than any vocalists I've heard.

John Scott (musician): The song I was aware of from that album was 'Dart', mainly because it had that dual vocal approach between lyric and chorus and so it wasn't just a single male vocal – in retrospect, I think that album featured more of Kellie's vocals as well, which I think was a strengthening of the band, providing them with a more variety and nuance.

Steve Bell: *Kitten Licks* was elevated. It was just like they all hit the top of their game at once. I even think that artwork's really important, for some reason it's like this perfect name and imagery. There's this innocence to it that really coloured your perception. If it was called *Ballcrusher* or something … Just this real warmth to the name and the artwork, in correlation with the slightly more polished sound.

Andrew P Street (journalist, musician): *Kitten Licks* is that perfect distillation of all the more hardcore-influenced stuff that came before (on previous records) and the growing realisation that the band's superweapon was their versatility, which would flower on (subsequent album) *Rocks on the Soul*. It sounds like a band really coming into their identity and discovering just how much they could do. And it's also the album that introduced Dean, which was a huge leap forward.

Chris Yates (musician): *Kitten Licks* was extremely exciting when it came out, it really felt like they were being appreciated and recognised on a national level which seemed like some small amount of justice in the world. The polish on the recording didn't detract from the authenticity of the sound, the songs are razor sharp, the wonderful artwork all just clicks it all into place.

Tim: That design of the animals came from this little tiny jumpsuit that was my daughter's when she was a zero. That little bird was on it. I can't remember if the kitten was on it, and Carl Breitkreuz illustrated more birds, but that's where the cover came from. We'd usually settle on the name super late, and it's almost always from the lyrics. [**Ben:** 'Dead to the World'?] Yes, exactly, that's where we got the title from. So I think I thought of that one or someone did, and we all went, *Yeah that'll do*. It's got a quite nice ring to it.

Darren Levin (*Mess+Noise*, 2009): I first heard *Kitten Licks* as a teenager in mid-1996, a time when Australian indie – stuck for so long in the quagmire of grunge – finally began to develop an identity of its own. Seattle's downcast posturing

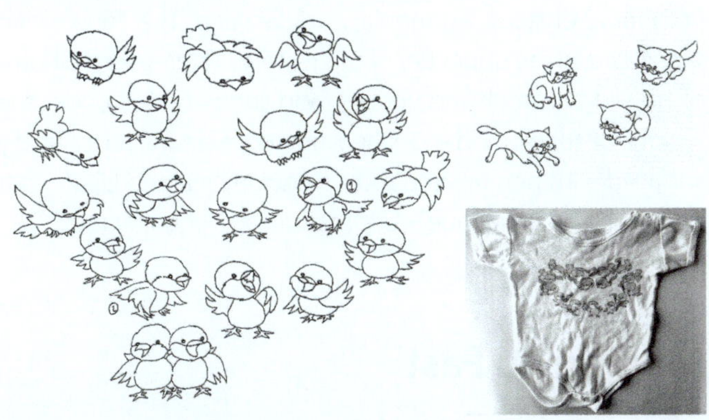

Figure 3 *Illustrations by Carl Breitkreuz (from facsimile held by the State Library of Queensland), with the baby jumpsuit that inspired them (photo courtesy of Tim Steward).*

had been replaced by a buoyant and effervescent pop, brimming with the kind of idiosyncrasies and cultural quirks that make music from this country so frustrating at times, but also so great. That it was released in the same year as You Am I's *Hourly Daily*, Regurgitator's *tu-plang*, Powderfinger's *Double Allergic*, Spiderbait's *Ivy and the Big Apples*, Magic Dirt's *Friends in Danger*, Bluebottle Kiss' *Fear of Girls* and The Fauves' *Future Spa*, was no coincidence. Radio support had re-energised a sleeping giant – and when 'Buy Me a Pony' (by Spiderbait) topped the Hottest 100, you really got the feeling that anything was possible again.[1] Whether conscious or not, *Kitten Licks*'s classic opener 'Static' was emblematic of this time.

Marcus Teague (*The Vine*, 2009): In a time when You Am I had virtually locked the door to the annals of Australian 'indie' music history from the inside, with a succession of killer number one albums (and that's back when hitting Number One meant something), bands *like* Screamfeeder were milling about the wings in their hundreds. (We can add groups like Pollyanna, Custard, Ammonia, Tumbleweed, The Fauves and Magic Dirt to the upper tier of this history.) After several albums of howling art rock and echoey pop songs buried under the weight of furious indie guitar wringing, Screamfeeder finally surfaced with perhaps the most singularly realized LP of – not just their own catalogue – but that decade of guitar rock.

Moving So Fast

Tim: I guess as always, we were trying to be as busy as we could and moving so fast that we didn't really take even one step back and go: *Oh, look at us, look what we've got, look what we've done.* We never did that ever. We were just head down, bum up, went for it and did it for ages.

Dean: Just a whole lot of playing, playing, playing, all the time. A lot of driving, a lot of flying. It was pretty good! I was just living by myself. At one point I was living next to Tim on Petrie Terrace in a one-bedroom unit, just a crummy old flat. Playing was all you wanted to do, really. There was nothing at home, so you'd just play as much as you can. I was young, with a lot of energy. I'd get on the beers and be fine the next day.

Kellie: It's a real blur. Constantly touring, playing with heaps of bands, playing all the big festivals. Being that band that's always supporting the bigger bands in the country. Just relentless touring.

Dean: Lots of Livids, Big Day Outs, Homebakes, and other random festivals that people were putting on. The festivals were always good shows. Good riders, good catering, just comfortable, kind of how gigs should be. They should all be how the Rolling Stones play. They've got their own cooks, don't they?

Kellie: One thing that I say to people who are starting to do a lot of stuff is, *Always try to just take a moment and really look at what's going on and think about where you are and appreciate it.* 'Cause we never did. And Tim and I have talked about this. Everything was happening, and it wasn't happening *to* us 'cause we were creating it, but you know, there was a record label, there was a manager, there was an agency booking everything and it just did become this thing that was happening to us. Record store signings and those kinds of weird things that happened in the 90s to bigger bands. We were becoming that bigger band. It was weird and scary, but it was happening, and we were just doing it.

Dean: There used to be TV ads for *Kitten Licks* on Channel Ten. So you'd be watching *Neighbours* and the ads would come on for *Kitten Licks*. I don't know why I was watching *Neighbours* but that's when they were doing it.

John Scott: My fond memory of Screamfeeder is Kellie, me, my brother Kim, along with Kram and Janet from Spiderbait all going bowling during a break in one of the tours. Our team won, I believe. Kellie and I shared a similar interest in authors and we also engaged in old-fashioned letter writing to one another, discussing serial killers and other dark subjects!

Damien Hughes (webmaster): They were very open to the idea of someone doing a website for them. If they were very standoffish and acted like rock stars I probably just would've said, *Nah, go fuck yourselves.* But Screamfeeder were never like that, they were always very welcoming to me and like, *Hey man, here's your name on the door, come to all the shows,* so I ended up doing that and tuning guitars for them and whatever. Just because I had that personal connection to them. I hadn't had that with any other band.

Tim: We're like the most amateur band ever, we're so unorganised and hopeless at everything that we didn't make the most of it at all. This was back in the day when we still would go on tour and have like one little box of t-shirts and we'd just stand there at the back with no light on, no signs, just in case anyone bought a t-shirt. *They're 20 bucks.* You know, *We sold three t-shirts tonight.* Even our own shows, I don't remember how we figured out the door price, but it was always mega cheap, five or ten bucks entry. We didn't really put much financial foresight or planning into things like that.

Kellie's Tour Diary 1997

NEW YEAR'S DAY Well, they say what you do on the first day of the year is an indication of what the year will hold for you. We spent the first day of 1997 in a Tarago heading south. A trip that takes 12 hours. A whole day, in a car with a hangover. I guess this year will be a big one! The journey was fairly non-descript, the tape selection was monotonous and repetitive – just the same as on all our other trips.

A new year's resolution is to get a totally different selection of tapes. Not just the usual 90's Grunge-a-Rama. God, you know I love Seam, but I think I'm going to hit someone if I have to listen to The Problem With Me in a confined space one more time! Only one speeding ticket this trip to Sydney. We kept to the speed limit remarkably well which resulted in a halved fuel bill. We're on our way to our first of the suburban Sydney shows with the Hoodoo Gurus, we play the Metro and then up the northern New South Wales Coast as the main support for the 'Gurus.

Radio, *rage* and *Recovery*

Tim: I guess at that point we were moving away from being associated with bands like Fur, Midget and Budd, which is the first half of the 90s. Moving into hanging out with bands like Spiderbait, Regurgitator and, never Powderfinger, but you know, Jebediah and those sort of Triple J bands. So we're really in that family of bands. I felt like we were a big family at that point 'cause we'd always see each other all the time and everyone would always be on tour.

Steve Bell: It was tangible. You'd see them on *Recovery* and you'd see them on *rage*, you'd hear about their escapades and they were at the vanguard of this really fertile Brisbane scene and that was definitely recognised at the time as well. There was a real spotlight on the Brisbane music scene and Screamfeeder were a part of that.

Joe Woolley: Everyone knows that they [Custard, Powderfinger, Regurgitator and Screamfeeder] were the big four bands that came out of Brisbane. The very big three and Screamfeeder. The other three were on major labels and Screamfeeder weren't. So it was all the more incomprehensible how they could be in that position. Without these loathsome people from Sydney with their big cheque books. It is amazing that it became that big of a record, but was put out through [independent distributor] Shock – which was pretty new at that stage, it wasn't big and it wasn't super well-established – it was amazing for them to have that kind of success and to be elevated to that sort of rarified echelon of Australian bands.

Tim (1998): Well we got a lot of interviews on mainstream radio stations, but … the album didn't quite do *that* well for us to be treated differently. I mean, a lot of people know us anyway because we've been around a long time and have quite a few albums out, not because we're this week's big sellers.[2]

Steve Bell: Every one of the singles off *Kitten Licks* was just like an earworm, and they sounded so great on radio.

Tim: Triple J was, at that time, amazing. Everything we put out, they'd pick up and we were so lucky. They probably played ten of our singles to death.

Darren Levin (2009): Our national youth broadcaster flogged *Kitten Licks* – and rightfully so. It was brimming with the kind of hooks that'd sell millions if Screamfeeder weren't so intent on doing things their own way.[3]

Tim: We went and did a live session with Triple J just after *Kitten Licks* came out, played a bunch of those songs. We just farted around and goofed off and we probably should have approached it a bit more professionally, but we were just on tour and so it was just a thing we did.

Kellie: We did *Recovery* like three times.

Tim: As much as it's amazing exposure, it looks great when you see it on telly and you're on TV around the whole country. But actually playing it is weird. There's no real foldback, there's miniature little speakers and you can't really hear yourself singing. You've got to play really quietly. And there's cameras everywhere and it's fucking 8 A.M. and you're hungover.

Kellie: You had to get there really early, like six in the morning. There was one night, I have a vague memory that we left very early in the morning from Ballarat, probably 4.30 or 5 o'clock in the morning to get there on time. We could only do it while we were on tour, we never just went to Melbourne to be on

Recovery. And most of the other bands that you saw on there that weren't from Melbourne, they would have been touring as well. Like I remember Fur were on there and they were still pretty drunk.

Dean: It's pretty warm, those bloody TV lights. You'd get in there early, maybe do a bit of a rehearsal, that'd be it until 9 o'clock comes. You'd do your two tracks. You'd stand around until your next track or whatever it is and then that's the end of the show and you get the hell out of there. Pretty good, pretty easy.

Kellie: It was such a great show. There's been nothing like it since, and nothing like it before either. But it is such a weird experience playing live because you're so far away from the audience. They throw to you and you're kind of like, *Oh, do we do this now?* And the cameras are moving around, they're in your face and you're trying to play a live show at like 8:30 or 9 o'clock in the morning. Dealing with your hangover appearing during the show because you'd have to play twice, maybe. Just feeling pretty bad, but you're in this incredible, historic moment.

Tim: There's that one with that dude dancing to us playing 'Hi C's'. He's this fucking maniac that we know who was like, *Oh yeah, I did this dance for Rocket from the Crypt* and all this. I'm like, *Yeah, you wanna come on TV with us tomorrow morning?* We shouldn't have done it. It's like halfway through the song and he's like (panting).

Kellie: We did the *rage* hosting thing. We were hungover and we started drinking and we got drunk again. We were eating popcorn. We were at someone I don't know's house, getting drunk, introducing songs that we weren't gonna see. I pronounced Will Oldham wrong, I called him Will Old-HAM and Tim's giggling in the background. How did they let this happen? I was wearing an awful shirt. Everything about it is awful. But we're very lucky to have that as part of our cultural history in Australia. There's nothing like that anywhere else, I don't think. It was an honour to do *rage*.

rage, August 1997 broadcast

Tim: *This next song's Hüsker Dü, 'Don't Wanna Know If You Are Lonely', and it comes from ten years ago – at least, maybe even more. And Hüsker Dü have always been a big sort of influence in our band anyway –*

Kellie: *[with mouthful of popcorn] Mmm.*

Tim: *We just all love em –*

Kellie: *Love Hüsker Dü.*

Tim: *They've got a great pop sort of feel about them even though they've managed to make it kind of, well abrasive for their time anyway, it's not really abrasive these days. They're one of the first bands who kind of came out of the punk scene and made punky sounding songs but with beautiful pop melodies. I think also they were way ahead of their time and influenced, just about everyone. [Discusses Pixies origin story involving Hüsker Dü]*

Kellie: *[Interrupting] Their music's really – um, you know, it's full-on music and then the lyrics are kind of even more full-on,* *sorta thing, like the music makes you wanna (jigging fists up and down) it kinda makes you happy cos it's like rockin' and rollin' and (laughs) fast and, you know really good, and then the lyrics make you wanna cry. They're really, you know, some of the lyrics are really …*

Tim: *But they're just such beautiful simple pop songs even though they're really sad. Like this is a song by Grant Hart, he's the drummer, he wrote all the more poppy edged kinda songs, and they're just concise and perfect and great.*

Dean: *[clears throat] Very –*

Tim: *Here it is.*

Dean: *Yeah.*

Recovery appearances

1996: Performing 'Static' and 'Bridge Over Nothing'.

August 1997: Performing 'Bruises' and 'Gravity'.

4 October 1997: Presenting a driving tour of Brisbane sights, soundtracked by 'Dart': the *XXXX* brewery, Lang Park stadium, the Story Bridge, Kangaroo Point cliffs, the Livid festival site under construction, and the ping pong table on Kellie's back deck. Kellie says to camera: 'There's never been that much known about Brisbane bands until recently – Regurgitator, Powderfinger, us, Custard.'

1998: Acting as 'house band', wearing feather boas, sunglasses, a dress for Tim, performing musical interstitial snippets of their own songs and others (e.g. a Kyuss riff).

7 November 1998: Performing 'Hi Cs' and 'Triple Hook'.

Radio polls

4ZZZfm Hot 100 1996 (Brisbane community radio listener poll)

1. Fish n Chip Bitch From Ipswich – Escape from Toytown
2. Dart – Screamfeeder
3. Static – Screamfeeder
4. Fuckhead Zone – Escape from Toytown
5. DSS – Small Fantasy
6. Kung Fu – Ash
7. Speculator – Insurge
8. Naked Eye – Luscious Jackson
9. Kong Foo Sing – Regurgitator
10. Thunder – Mavis's

…

16. No KFC – Scrumfeeder [Brisbane punk band formed in 1995, with a name punning on Screamfeeder and a love of rugby league football]

…

28. Buy me a Pony – Spiderbait [#1 in that year's Triple J Hottest 100]

…

41. Bridge Over Nothing – Screamfeeder [never released as a single]

'The Hottest 100 songs to have missed triple j's Hottest 100 (#102 – 200)' (Tyler Jenke, *Tone Deaf*, 2021)

172. Static – Screamfeeder

6 Consistently Intermittent

Survival and Sustainability

*The post-*Kitten Licks *era of Screamfeeder is one partially defined by inactivity and business machinations. A bad American record deal destroyed the band's momentum in the late 90s, effectively closing off the lucrative international market as a career avenue. This century, the band bounced back hard. To date, Screamfeeder have released three studio albums, an EP, two best-of albums (2004's* Introducing: Screamfeeder *and 2011's* Patterns Form*) and a collection of b-sides. Not bad for a band that was intermittently inactive throughout parts of the 2000s and 2010s. In terms of official album releases, they followed up* Kitten Licks *with a very different record:* Rocks on the Soul *(2000). Produced by Melbourne-based duo The Pound System,* Rocks on the Soul *incorporated lush, electronic elements. Shoegaze sounds feature prominently. The album worked, acquiring warm reviews and Triple J support, but their follow-up to* Kitten Licks *did not return the band to the commercial peak of that previous record. In 2001, Darek Mudge joined the band as a live guitarist, later becoming a full member. Then in 2003, Screamfeeder released* Take You Apart *(2003), returning to a more rough-hewn sound. It would be another fourteen years before* Pop Guilt *(2017) arrived, and another five years before 2022's* Five Rooms*, their most recent album. Around these records, they toured. Between the various*

Closing America

Tim: There's a weird period that ensued after the whole American deal. The American *Kitten Licks* came out in '97, '98, I can't remember [1999 – see *Selected Discography*].

Tim (1998): Well we've been going to practice four times a week and writing and rehearsing new songs. We've got quite a bunch now, and are going to record them in April for our new album. Ken Stringfellow from the Posies is going to come and record it for us!

[email addendum to interview] OK, we were going to be recording with Ken from The Posies starting on the 23rd of April, for two weeks. We have recently heard that an American record label is seriously interested in the band. They seem to be a real, proper committed label, unlike Taang, who we got shafted by a few years back. They want us to go to the states and record, tour, everything, and they're prepared to put up a far more substantial recording budget than Shock are able to. So, the Ken session has been canned. It's a bummer for now, as the release of the album here is going to be delayed further.[1]

Kellie: This is how close it was. We signed to Taang! before this other label and they were like *Yeah, we're going to bring you over.* They put out *Burn Out Your Name* and I changed all my money into US dollars and travellers cheques and then the [label] guy's credit card bounced and the tickets didn't come through. And it all got thrown into disarray, the whole thing was cancelled. Then later came the Time Bomb thing, so a second time in America, someone at a label totally fucked us up. Against our manager's advice we signed the contract and fucked it all up. They were all excited about *Kitten Licks* and they had plans to put 'Dart' out through college radio.

Tim: In the interim they said, *You can't record a new album in Australia. You gotta wait.* Even back then they were like, *It'll get leaked on the Internet and we'll lose potential revenue.* That was their reason.

Tim (1999): We've got a new record deal in the workings and we're waiting for all the contractual bullshit to be sorted out and all the legal and financial and that kinda crap to go down before we can record. Coz the new label is going to finance it for us, and they're gonna give us a big budget to do it with so it's worth waiting for, even tho' every day goes past it's becoming more a pain in the arse …[2]

Kellie: They put out 'Dart' first as a single and it didn't quite do what they expected, so they didn't know what to do and they just shrugged and went, *Next.* And then they wouldn't release us from the contract that said we couldn't do anything in this country. That's why there's this massive break.

Tim: And so we toured the shit out of *Kitten Licks*. If I managed a band that put out and did that, I'd be like, *Right, you fucking gotta get in the studio, whatever it takes, and make another album that's that good NOW!* You gotta roll with it, and we didn't. We let it drop because of that stupid American thing – partially, but still. Making that American thing happen was a waste of time and energy and burnt up a whole lot of time that we should have used more productively.

Kellie: We still worked really hard but we didn't just slog it out. We stopped playing regionally. With the next album, we started flying because it was, maybe, getting to the point where we were burning out on the road. We'd nearly died a couple of times by hitting kangaroos or swerving onto the wrong side of the road half asleep. It just got too frightening. Flying became the way we'd go on tour. We'd fly to the major cities and we'd fly home and just be away for the weekend. Then I needed to get a job. I just got a succession of shit jobs to pay the rent and continue. We lost all that momentum. *Kitten Licks* was our biggest record, and we had toured it as much as we could and we were stuck. I don't know what would have happened if we were not signed to this American label and we'd done the next record. Which wouldn't have been the next record, because we would have written different songs. Potentially we would have rushed an album and fallen over anyway.

Tim: We've got a bunch of songs sitting there that we've never done anything with, demos. Not awesome ones, but there's probably ten songs which never came out.

Kellie: I would like to know what the sliding doors moment would be, if we did do our next record within two years, and who would we have done it with then? What would those songs be like and what would have happened? But I don't know, maybe having that break meant that we changed direction a bit and that's when everything started to change too. It was 2000 when we put out our next record. It was not the 90s anymore.

Surviving *Kitten Licks*

Ian Rogers (*Rocks on the Soul* liner notes): To become a teacher where I work, you have to write a PhD thesis. I wrote mine on Brisbane music. I spoke to about twenty-five musicians – which doesn't sound like many – but it was enough. In Brisbane, that represents one hundred bands. And the 'data' was raw. One interviewee had to take sedatives, just to talk about the past. Another got so wasted during our interview that the tape is almost three hours long. Most of these interviews were conducted with scrappy indie rock bands (thus the dysfunction) so they all talked about Screamfeeder. They're the yardstick everyone used.

Ian Rogers (PhD thesis excerpt): For the hobbyist musician and the emerging music professional, failure is never far from view … it is almost always approaching, bringing with it subtle and not-so-subtle reminders of just how abstract the rock dream is.

Tim (1998): The whole indie ethic has gone down the toilet, in fact bands which we would still call 'indie' are shunted way out to the sidelines. But, on the other hand, we're simply not making top 40 music, like these young bands are. We're making music which is valid and important to *us*.[3]

Kellie: I remember when I read the book, *Our Band Could Be Your Life* [by Michael Azerrad]. It's just about people making decisions to do things a certain way. And Tim and I have always tried to make all the right decisions, but we only ever followed our hearts and did what we thought was right. Never kind of sold out, never tried to do anything to make stuff for other people, it was always for us. And then listening to these records I feel like we've really accomplished that. We were true to ourselves.

Kellie (1999): It's always been the big conflict. We really like being able to play small venues and have a really cool audience, like we could talk to every single person in that audience and have a good conversation. But once you've got a really massive, huge audience, you just see so many fuckwits there you'd just think, *I don't wanna play for these people*.[4]

Tim (1998): I think we went through that big frustration thing a year or two ago, when *Kitten Licks* had been out for a while, and nothing really changed. But we're over that now. It's like, we know that we like what we're doing.[5]

Kellie: When we met our early manager [Joe Segreto], I told him, 'I don't want to be a big rock star.' I don't want to have what happened to Ratcat happen to us.[6]

Tim: When we went on tour in the early days, prior to Dean joining the band, we'd play somewhere like the Punters Club or whatever, and we'd get like three grand at the end of the night in fifty dollar notes. We'd go *Fuck, that's amazing!* And then by the time we got home and paid some for advertising, paid for the van, the petrol, maybe some recording, it was always gone. But when *Kitten Licks* came out things were better. We went on tour with Regurgitator and Spiderbait, and we were probably getting, like, 1000 bucks a night, clear. So we would have some pocket money for sure. We would come home and have two grand or three grand each. But that doesn't last more than a couple of weeks really. It's not exactly living off the band. So there were those moments where it was good, and the rest of the time it's like the band account is hovering around zero.

Kellie: When we were doing all the heavy touring, I was working casual jobs, as well as going on and off the dole every so often. There was one point when we did this Hoodoo Gurus tour up the east coast and I went off the dole and I got paid and all that money got stolen. Like backstage at a gig. It was freaking awful. But that was the only time I was employed by the band and the rest of the time I was just like working in the library, working in a courier place, working at a pasta factory. I worked all these weird jobs and eventually it was like *I need to get a real job*. I'm a smart person, I did a film degree, y'know.

Dean: *Kitten Licks* kept us playing, and kept people coming to gigs and it didn't really die off until the early 2000s. I think rock in general started fading a bit around then. You know, I can't remember. I don't know. What is the record after that, was it *Take You Apart?* I can't remember.

Pressing On

Kellie: We did have to stop and re-enter the world. I worked at QUT [Queensland University of Technology] library for a couple of years I think at that point, I felt a bit lost and did a lot of binge drinking and going out and seeing other bands and, you know, doing all that stuff. I hadn't really been home for ages. So that was interesting and a bit sad and a bit weird. But then we were always still looking ahead, like *we gotta do the next record.*

Darek Mudge: I grew up in Townsville, and the live music scene up there was pretty much dead. My first concert was silverchair and Regurgitator, in 1996. I never saw Screamfeeder until I moved to Brisbane in 2000, to study at [audio school] SAE. I only really got to know Screamfeeder because my lecturer at SAE was Paul Daly [who would later join Tim in We All Want To]. He was really good friends with them, and around that same time they were looking for a new guitarist. He suggested I try out for the band. He called Tim on his landline from his office at SAE and put me on the spot. *I got this dude, he wants to play guitar for you.* I was kinda forced into it. They invited me around to Dean's house to have a cup of tea and a bit of a discussion. I was living in Paddington, and it turned out that Dean lived directly across the road from me. I just walked across the road, had this meeting and then they gave me a couple of CDs with seven or eight songs to learn. It was pretty exciting. I was twenty.

Ian Rogers (*Rocks on the Soul* liner notes): Kellie told me about the band's stretch of commercial success around *Kitten Licks* and about quitting her day job, touring in vans and airplanes and what came after. She told me about all the different ways that America didn't work out for Screamfeeder and – looking at the minutiae of those stories in the transcripts – I think some of these stories are the sort that people never recover from, let alone bands.

Kellie: I'm kind of thankful that what happened, happened. Because we didn't go to the States and we didn't implode over there, or have a car accident and die, or whatever could have happened. I kind of feel like there was a reason why we didn't. And I'm really happy with that, because we did get to make that next record and it did end up being what it was [*Rocks on the Soul*, 2000]. Because a record is a record of that moment and all the people that worked on it and the songs and what happened that day. So, you know, I'm really proud of all of the things and I wouldn't change it.

Ian Rogers (PhD thesis excerpt): The rock dream starts out broad and impressionistic and is whittled down to a more manageable set of goals by experience. Visions of success set limits, they demarcate what is possible and how it is to be achieved. Failure narrows these goals even further; it is a process by which everyday life is gradually re-incorporated into the rock dream. It is the mechanism by which more experienced musicians make concessions and reassess their aspirations.

Kellie: We had an interruption. Dean went overseas for a few years, and we sort of stopped playing, but Tim and I still kept playing duet shows or, you know, whatever we could do. And Tim and Dean did THE WHATS [side-project]. And later on, Tim did We All Want To [side-project]. I did like four other bands [including Warm Guns, White Mansions and A Savage God], solo stuff. We're all really ambitious, or just really creatively pushed, or whatever it is. And then we would always come back together and go, *It's so much easier with you*. We just know how to work together, and I think maybe one of the things about that is the fact that Tim and I were never romantically involved. There are lots of bands where a girl in the band is dating somebody, then when they break up, the band break up. We've never had that, which is uh … it's an interesting dynamic that some people really can't understand.

Tim Rogers (musician): I couldn't foresee that after periods where the band were not performing they would cleave together, cleave apart, making vital, yearning music. And when apart, get other wonderful combos together, be perennially supportive and encouraging of others attempting to eke out an opportunity to play, and live as they exist as a band – ethically, passionately … spiritually.[7]

Joe Woolley: I've been having the same conversation with booking agents and venue people for ten years: *Can I explain to you we don't have support bands that don't have women in them?* We don't. You'll never see one. Doesn't happen. We don't shout about it. We just go, *These are our values*. We just ask you to respect them. So they're very humble, very clear. Probably the key attribute that is shared across Screamfeeder is they are all very humble. You never hear them say, *Hang on, we're Screamfeeder. That's not good enough*, or *We deserve this*. We don't demand things, we don't say we deserve things. We just very quietly have a word to people and go, *It would be really nice if we could do that.*

Kellie: We were really serious. And you know, Tony [Blades] was very serious about the band. He'd come home from working all day and sit on the phone all night talking to Wally Meanie [from Melbourne punk band The Meanies] about touring Victoria and setting up tours and doing artwork. And I did feel really bad I'd taken away his band. And he didn't do another band after that. He sold his gear and eventually moved to Germany.

Joe Woolley: These days, Tim is the nominal boss. Tim does more of the work than anyone else. I don't think anyone will argue with that. He puts in a significant amount of work on the band, and you know, does all the merch, and he works a lot. But Kellie is the one that can say no. If you want a yes from Screamfeeder, you have to get a yes from Kellie. And a yes from Tim is not a final yes, 'cause Kellie can say no. And Kellie does say that. I would say politically and socially, they have a very clear idea of the kind of things that they can do and should do. Which is good, 'cause they get asked a lot of things, so I get to say no to a lot of stuff that they get asked to do. But occasionally something will come along and I'll go, *That might fit.* So they will do a free show for Reclink [Community Cup charity Australian Rules football match], they'll do a free show for Stop Adani [movement to stop the Adani Carmichael coal mine, rail and port project in Queensland], they'll do a free show for a women's refuge. There are things that I know that I'll say to them, *You're not going to get any money,* and they go, *Yeah, that fits with what we want to do.*

Tim: Every time I hear *Kitten Licks*, I'm happy with it and I don't cringe over it and I don't wish anything different about it and it makes me remember that period very fondly. So, it's really lovely that people still care about. It's amazing.

Ian Rogers (*Rocks on the Soul* liner notes): Everyone I knew was playing in bands but no one had been doing it as long as Screamfeeder. No one had as many stories. No one probably would.

7 Some Mysterious Transaction

Remembering *Kitten Licks*

The idea, like so many others, grew from idle chatter and jokes. The members of Screamfeeder had observed the resurgence of Nineties bands and the Don't Look Back *concert series, which brought the phenomenon of 'classic albums live' to the alternative music world. Cult favourites were played for bigger audiences (and sums) than some artists had ever seen the first time around. In 2007, the reunited Pixies headlined a festival at the Gold Coast; in 2008, Sonic Youth came to Australia for the last time to perform* Daydream Nation (1988) *in full. In 2009, Screamfeeder played* Kitten Licks *from start to finish in Brisbane's 200-odd capacity venue The Troubadour. This quickly grew into a national tour, a deluxe CD reissue (through Melbourne's Low Transit Industries), and a nostalgic rush from critics and fans. Such events were still a novelty, certainly at this level, and the thirteen-year-old album held the status of a widely cherished but somehow underrated classic. The band committed to the project – Kellie played 'Helen's Theme' on a keyboard between 'Ant' and 'End of the Wire', a saxophonist joined them for 'Pigtails on a Rock' – and so did their audience. The shows were triumphant love-ins.*

In 2014, Melbourne independent label Poison City Records began reissuing the first five Screamfeeder albums on vinyl, spurring more stage dives into the deep catalogue. Before long, it was the thirtieth anniversary of the band, and the twenty-fifth anniversary of Kitten Licks. *The 2020s have seen the consolidation of a 1990s Australian alt-rock nostalgia circuit, with the Homebake bands reunited at mini-festivals on winery grounds. Screamfeeder are a winning conversation starter in the 20,000-strong Facebook group,* Sound As Ever (Australian Indie 90–99). *In 2022, they played all of* Kitten Licks *again, this time in a different order, alongside Regurgitator revisiting* Tu-Plang *in a joint Brisbane quarter-century special (delayed one year by a pandemic). Songs from* Kitten Licks *also endure in regular setlists, and sometimes the first three tracks are strung together for an unfailing thrill. Likewise, Screamfeeder as a band and as people remain constants of the local Brisbane scene, and the trans-local network of music scenes that thrive around the country. Generations of bands and fans admire them as much as, and in large part* because, *they relate to them. Kellie is a particular inspiration to the growing number of women and gender-diverse people pursuing music, and Tim is the model of a lifer: prolific and passionate.*

Kellie: *Kitten Licks* changed our lives. It brought us together as the band we are today. It had an impact on a lot of other people too. Over the years it's been noted that this is the album we'll be remembered for; it was our most successful in terms of sales and was widely acclaimed, it got us a whole legion of new fans, opened up our worlds and sent us out touring Australia solidly for a couple of years.[1]

Darren Levin (2009): How can one album transcend the zeitgeist and yet be utterly of its time? Hearing Screamfeeder's *Kitten Licks* again is a transportive experience, like watching a film you loved as a kid or flipping through an old album of family photos. It instantly conjures memories of eyebrow rings and bottle dye, of waking up early for *Recovery* and staying up late to watch *rage*. It makes judging a reissue like this on musical merits alone a difficult ask, because it's wrapped up in the kind of nostalgia that irons out all kinks.[2]

Andrew Hayden (owner/founder Poison City Records): I was a huge Screamfeeder fan. Since my high school years, those early Screamfeeder records were so ingrained in my musical journey and had probably opened my ears to crucial US indie bands like Hüsker Dü, Pavement and Sonic Youth. With my music-obsessed journey eventually leading me to starting my own indie record label (Poison City) in the early 2000s I had always daydreamed about contacting some of my 90s underground music heroes with suggestions of re-issuing albums that might be out of print, lost along the way or simply had never made it onto vinyl. I remember being up late doing emails one night, with *Kitten Licks* playing the background when I had the sudden impulse to email Tim with the idea of a vinyl re-issue series of those early Screamfeeder albums. Although I'd seen Screamfeeder play a bunch of times over the years, I'd never actually met Tim, Kellie or Dean in person, so being somewhat of a cold call, I was mentally preparing for little or no response. Of course, as it turns out Tim was a total sweetheart, calling me the next day and saying they loved the idea. Fortunately for me, Tim also turned out to be a meticulous archiver of Screamfeeder masters, artwork, flyers, photos – so pulling together the artwork and arranging vinyl remastering proved smooth sailing. It still blows my mind that a band that I've admired since my formative high school years are now close friends and I was able to play a small part in their journey. I've actually laughed about this with Kellie recently – but thinking back to high school days, I even had a magazine cut out of her, Link Meanie and Dean/Magic Dirt on my school folder at some stage – thanks *Hot Metal* magazine!

Tim (2009): It was funny though, we got together and listened to the new edition of the album, with all the b-sides. Suddenly after the final track 'Pigtails on a Rock' ended, there was another song – slam! – called 'Harlan'. Kellie almost pissed herself, she hadn't even heard it since 1997.[3]

Kellie: I listened to the album with Tim when it came, when we got it on vinyl and was really … I hadn't listened to it for ages. And, I mean, lots of people say how it's such a huge part of their lives. It's the soundtrack of their early 20s or whatever. And I'm like, *Yeah, that's great.* I wish I knew what that was like. But I have my own records that were the soundtrack of my life at that time.

Tim: There was a reissue in 2009 through Low Transit Industries. That was a CD which had bonus tracks as well. And then we did the 2014 Poison City ones, and now [2022] we've got a new Poison City/ Modern Morning co-release, and that's just 'cause we ran out of the stock of the 2014 one. Four releases. That's crazy. Twenty-five years on. Fuuuuck.

'Make a *Kitten Licks*'

Steve Bell: In the 2000s when I started working with bands, managing bands and with the label, that's when I really noticed that Screamfeeder, and *Kitten Licks* in particular, was a bit of a touchstone for the next generation of bands. There's certain songs that remind me of a petrol station in New South Wales or a highway, because we were always playing it in the van. It's hard sometimes to get people in a van to agree, but chuck on *Kitten Licks* and everyone was like (claps) *Sweet!* singing along more often than not. It could have been Giants of Science or Iron On or Intercooler, everyone loved *Kitten Licks*. The Dollar Bar guys were huge fans. It seemed as if this album, to me, was a testament to the fact that you can be really successful on your own terms. And there was this awesome bit of art that had come out from a scene not different to what they were doing and that it was possible to … make a *Kitten Licks*!

Kate Cooper: I heard Screamfeeder on Triple J but I didn't have the record. It wasn't until I became good mates with Ross [Hope, Iron On singer/guitarist] that I truly discovered the record. He owned the CD and played it for me and I was blown away. I remember thinking *and these guys are from Brisbane? NO WAY! Maybe one day I can make a record as good as this and even play with them.* I am pretty sure Ross and I learnt how to sing together by singing along to that record. He would sing Tim's part and I would sing Kellie's. We would drive around Brisbane in my car in the sweltering heat, screaming our lungs out to their music. Kind of indignant to the rest of the world, just reveling in the sweet, sweet music from this band from Brisbane! So there was that extra layer of pride and respect. I remember [Brisbane guitar and record shop] Tym Guitars talking about how they made it to the United States and I remember thinking I have to do that!

Seja Vogel: As a teenager in Brisbane in the 90s, we were really lucky to have lots of all ages shows to go to and it felt like Screamfeeder were quite ubiquitous to an indie rock kid listening to (community radio station) Triple Zed, going to market day and watching ABC's *Recovery*. To me they were one of the biggest bands in Australia and I was really proud that they were from my home town. I owe a lot to Screamfeeder. Not only did they take my band Sekiden out on tour, Tim gave our tape to Steve Pavlovic (Modular Records, tour promoter) with some kind words which helped get us signed to the label. On tour they really took us under their wing and we became fast friends. It's so nice when your musical heroes end up living up to their hero status in real life. I also learnt a lot from Kellie about touring in the predominantly male-heavy industry in the 90s. It was so important to me to have female camaraderie at that time and I really cherished touring with her. Kellie, Kate Cooper from Iron On and I also had a little support group that would meet for coffee after one of us had finished a big tour to help battle the post-tour-blues and bring each other gently back down to earth.

Alex Campbell: I love grunge, and I remember listening to it and just thinking how cool that we had this amazing grunge band from Meanjin [name for Brisbane derived from the language of the Turrbal people, traditional owners along with the Jagera people]. I remember thinking that I'd never really heard anything like it before. The songs and lyrics were so catchy and melodic they were almost pop songs! And the lyrics are super profound. But it was heavy too, and the perfect amount of angst for a teenager, ha ha. It was important for me at the time (as a baby musician) to hear other voices in bands besides men, to know that women and non-binary people could make sick music too and be successful. Screamfeeder has definitely influenced my song writing, both early on being in grunge and punk bands, but also recently in my chiller bands. Also just generally, seeing myself as capable of playing this kind of music, and that it was worth it giving it a go wouldn't have been possible without seeing people like Kellie paving the way.

Andrew Hayden: Coming from my early teenage years where I'd gone from being a metal kid into Slayer, Metallica, Napalm Death, then discovering the more 'melodic rock' world of 90s Australian (and Seattle) bands (Mudhoney, Magic Dirt, Nirvana, Screaming Trees), Screamfeeder and more specifically *Kitten Licks* seemed to draw me in further, with an added lyrical depth and a more unique 'off kilter' sound I could never quite nail down. Knowing Tim and Kellie pretty well these days, I can appreciate their roots being in punk/ art-rock/ noisier type bands, but I know they also lean towards classic song writing and pop sensibility. For my particular taste in rock music, *Kitten Licks* walks that perfect line of clever indie rock song writing, while still maintaining that sense of 'punk' urgency, emotion, noise and unpredictability. Since working with Screamfeeder on that re-issue series, it's been a total pleasure getting to know them as the wonderful supportive people they are. We've hosted them at numerous gigs/ events in Melbourne and nice to have people to catch up with in Brisbane. Growing up and learning bass myself, Kellie and Dean [Turner] from Magic Dirt were always my favourite rock bass players – so it's still pretty wild to me that I've even played in a band (Majestic Horses) with Kellie in recent years. Most of our musical tastes expand and contract as we move through life, but there's always those special bands/ albums that stick right by you.

Kate McGuire: The first time I heard the band was when 'Dart' came on in my 'Discover Weekly' [Spotify playlist]. I fell in love immediately. It was everything I wanted out of the alt-rock bands I knew and loved without it being so obvious and world-popular. I liked that about Screamfeeder. They did everything I wanted but still kept me on my toes.

Chris Yates: Screamfeeder are such an inspiration and a good news story for the fact they have done it their own way for so long, continuing to craft wonderful new songs and playing live. *Kitten Licks* may have been the moment where they slotted in neatly to the cultural zeitgeist of popular alternative music, but the fact they keep on delivering under their own steam is incredible.

Hardcore Fans

Tim: Screamfeeder's never been massively popular but the fans that we've got are quite hardcore. And there's people around the world who write to us and have travelled to Australia to meet us and things like that. And they're the loveliest people and they're the exact kinda people we want to draw into our little family, you know? It's like this beautiful thing. It's really nice.

Alex Campbell: When my band got asked to play with Tim's other band We All Want To it was a pretty crazy moment as a big fan. Same thing happened when I met Kellie at 4ZZZ one time, I got a bit silly.

Kate McGuire: Shortly after discovering the band and falling in love with them, Kellie and I started chatting over instagram. One day she sent me an old photo of her when she was in her early twenties saying I reminded her of herself when she was my age. Obviously after becoming such a big fan this was the coolest message to receive. One of the first times we met we got coffee and she told me heaps of stories about playing with Sonic Youth and Pavement, it was the coolest. Then she gave me original CDs of all their albums. I felt very special.

Kate Cooper: They remind me of a different period of my life. They are incredible songwriters who put on a great show. They feel like one of the most Brisbane things about Brisbane and for that I love them. *Kitten Licks* still crushes to this day. The production is classic, the songs are so strong and they just keep coming.

Kellie: We had a gig in Melbourne at a place called Applecore which is a backyard festival. It was raining and it was under a cover but it was all leaking down the side so we said, *Everybody get up on stage and get dry*. We were playing our song 'Dart' and the people who organised the show filmed it, but then in the middle of it, the guy asked his girlfriend to marry him as he was filming it. And so the next year they were married at the festival. It was really cool.

Joe Woolley: There are lots of bands that I like. There's only a few that I'm obsessed with. Screamfeeder fans are the ones that are obsessed with the band. They go and see every show, they buy every t-shirt – multiple of – they buy the hoodies, they buy the books. These people are really loyal and the band is their secret. So when you're walking down the street and you've got a Screamfeeder t-shirt on, if someone knows who that band is, they are a fan and they will stop and talk to you.

Andrew P Street: They're a band who never got bad. They've tried so many things, there's so much variety in their catalogue, and they're one of the most consistently excellent singles bands Australia has ever produced. And yet they're still a wonderful secret for everyone that loves them.

Living with *Kitten Licks*

Tim: It's easy to play because it's our most played bunch of songs. So we just go to practice and like our bodies just play the songs.

Darek: I love that it has different guitar tunings. It has a unique sound because of that. A lot of the time I'm just playing what Tim's playing on the record. If there's a lead part and he's singing, I'll usually take that on.

Dean: I was on a job a few years back and someone was in a unit doing their thing, and they had their stereo going. And I think Soundgarden came on, then like I think Pearl Jam came on, and then Screamfeeder, a song off *Kitten Licks* came on. And it just kind of fit in, like it didn't sound out of place, it sounded just as good as those. And you go, *Hold on*, you just stand there and you go, *That's fucking US!*

Tim: I barely ever listen to *Kitten Licks* but I did before the practices for the anniversary tour. It sounds awesome, I love it and I was really happy to hear it actually. There's no dud songs for me, I like playing them all. And listening back, I would always listen to the lyrics and the guitar 'cause it's my thing, but listening back years later I think, *Fuck the drummer is doing some cool shit there!*

Kellie: I was driving up and down the coast a bit for work and I made a playlist of the set that we were playing. I was able to listen as a non-critical listener, without trying to remember what the chords were, or listening to what the mix was like, or for mastering. And you know, I'd never really listened to our music as a casual listener. And I really, really enjoyed it. And I felt like really proud of it. And I think there was one point where I did just listen to *Kitten Licks* on its own in its entirety, doing nothing else but listening. And I messaged Tim and said, *Wow, we made a really great record*, you know? I'd never … I hadn't thought about it. It's just been the thing that we do.

8   If I Transmit Long Enough

One cold winter night in 2022, Screamfeeder are booked for a show in Melbourne at the Northcote Social Club. The city is still in the recovery position. Locked inside for almost half of the two-year COVID pandemic era, Melbourne's music fans are slow to re-emerge. Gigs still feel high-risk and ticket sales are sluggish across the board. When Screamfeeder announced their tour, it seemed ambitious for everyone involved: Would it actually happen? Would anyone turn up? Won't we all get sick again? Yet the show goes ahead.

The room is full. A humid mass of bodies, half of them in surgical masks. Looking around, most of the punters are middle-aged and coupled-up. Old friends meeting face-to-face once again. The babysitters of the inner-north must have been booked solid, just to get us here, into this room so we can surreally stand in the dark watching local band Moody Beaches and alt-icon Adalita (of fellow 90s rock act Magic Dirt) play their opening sets.

And then the drinks took hold and Screamfeeder started.

They opened with a long, new track 'Late to the Party'. It's one of the shoegaze numbers. A Kellie song. And it's not even halfway done when it becomes apparent that they're here, playing for us, because this is as important to them as it is to the audience.

There's no riding the goodwill, though. They work at it.

New and old tracks keep coming.

Down the front, a fifty-year-old man starts punching the air and playing air-guitar, hammered in a way that screams wine-drunk, and we all feel a piece of his mania, like every minute is slipping us closer to that kind of outpouring. Rage out or cry. Maybe both.

They play a bunch of *Kitten Licks* tracks.

'Static' into 'Dart'.

Then after twenty songs, they're done.

Back outside in the cold, waiting on an Uber, there's a couple who have just seen the band for the first time. They talk about how first-rate Screamfeeder sounds in 2022, how 90s and indie they are. *Where have they been all this time? Are they famous here?* They watched the show with fresh eyes. They love how Kellie is in the middle and how there's a heat coming off her. She feels classic to them. Alt-rock, clearly. A call back to the tone of that moment. Tim, on the other hand, reminds them of Hüsker Dü, and one of them has seen Bob Mould a few times. Just before they walk away, one of them says that Tim looks like he's a marathon runner. That works, right? These two didn't have the history, or all the records, but didn't miss anything, did they? They got the whole story, just from listening to the music.

Cast of Characters

Steve Bell: Music writer, street press editor and podcaster. Bell has managed bands, worked in music retail and founded Rhythm Ace Records (home to Screamfeeder's album *Take You Apart* in 2003).

Tony Blades: Founding member of The Madmen and Screamfeeder. Drummer with significant responsibility for bookings and organisation until his departure from the band in 1995.

Alex Campbell: Brisbane musician, 4ZZZ announcer and zine-maker. She is singer and guitarist in Full Power Happy Hour and Gunk.

Kate Cooper: Musician. Kate Cooper was a founding member of Brisbane indie band Iron On and now performs as An Horse.

Andrew Hayden: Musician and store/label owner of Poison City Records. Poison City reissued a number of Screamfeeder albums on vinyl.

Damien Hughes: Screamfeeder fan, occasional guitar tech and webmaster of Screamfeeder's first webpage. Producer of The Long Gone Loser Rock Show podcast and YouTube channel.

Jamie Hutchings: Lead singer-songwriter and guitarist for Bluebottle Kiss. He also records and performs as a solo artist.

Darren Levin: Music writer and editor, working across a variety of publications, including *Mess + Noise* and *Junkee Media*.

Kellie Lloyd: Founding member of Screamfeeder. Bass guitar player, vocalist and songwriter. Kellie also records and performs as a solo artist and in projects such as Majestic Horses and Deafcult.

Kate McGuire: Brisbane musician, guitarist and vocalist in VOIID and Mouse.

Paul McKercher: Australian record producer, audio engineer, multi-instrumentalist and teacher. He recorded and produced *Kitten Licks* alongside a notable collection of 1990s Australian rock bands, such as Screamfeeder contemporaries, Tumbleweed, Magic Dirt and You Am I.

Craig Mathieson: Australian music journalist and writer. Author of *Hi Fi Days* (1996), *The Sell-In* (2000) and *Playlisted: Everything You Need to Know About Australian Music Right Now* (2009).

Mary Mihelakos: Australian music promoter and journalist. Editor of Australian street paper *Beat Magazine* between 1995 and 2005.

Tom Morgan: Australian musician and songwriter. A founding member of Smudge (1991–present) and a songwriting contributor to Evan Dando's outfit The Lemonheads. He remains active in a number of music projects.

Darek Mudge: Screamfeeder guitarist. Performed live shows with the band since the *Rocks on the Soul* era and later joined the band in the studio for subsequent albums. Also a member of Brisbane band Intercooler and We All Want To with Tim Steward.

Tim Rogers: Musician. Tim Rogers is singer-guitarist for Australian rock band You Am I.

Dean Shwereb: Screamfeeder drummer. Currently on leave from the band (at the time of writing), but played on every Screamfeeder album from 1991 onward, starting with *Kitten Licks*.

John Scott: Musician. John Scott has recorded and performed with Adelaide rock band The Mark of Cain since 1984.

Joe Segreto: Screamfeeder's manager in the 1990s. Founder of IMC Agency and Homebake festival.

Andrew Stafford: Freelance journalist and author of *Pig City: From the Saints to Savage Garden* (2004) and *Something to Believe In* (2019).

Andrew P. Street: Author, journalist and musician. Alongside a diverse media career, Andrew performs in Majestic Horses with Kellie Lloyd.

Tim Steward: Founding member of Screamfeeder. Guitar player, vocalist and songwriter. Tim also played in THE WHATS (with Dean) and We All Want To and records and performs as a solo artist.

Marcus Teague: Musician, freelance music writer and editor. Marcus is the primary songwriter behind Melbourne band Deloris, in addition to numerous side-projects.

Seja Vogel: Musician and podcaster. Seja records and performs as a solo artist and for many years was a founding member of Brisbane band Sekiden. She has also performed in Regurgitator.

Joe Woolley: Screamfeeder's manager and owner/operator of Alien Lane Management.

Chris Yates: Musician, music writer and fan. He has performed with Dollar Bar, Shrapnel and a number of other projects.

Selected Discography

Albums and EPs

Flour (Survival, 1992)

Burn Out Your Name (Survival, 1993)

Felicitator EP (Survival, 1994)

Fill Yourself with Music (Hypnotized, 1995)

Kitten Licks (Hypnotized, 1996)

Home Age (Hypnotized, 1999)

Rocks on the Soul (Hypnotized, 2000)

Take You Apart (Rhythm Ace, 2003)

Delusions of Grandchildren EP (Bad Cop Recordings, 2005)

Pop Guilt (Four Four/ABC Music, 2017)

Five Rooms (Modern Morning, 2022)

Kitten Licks singles

'Static' (Hypnotized, 1996)

'Dart' (Hypnotized, 1996)

'Gravity' (Hypnotized, 1996)

Kitten Licks reissues

Time Bomb Recordings, 1999 – for this US release on CD and cassette, the tracklist was changed: b-side 'Summertime' replaces 'Dead To The World', 'Broken Ladder' is removed and 'Static' is remixed. 'Dart' was distributed as a promo-only radio single.

Low Transit Industries, 2009 – deluxe CD with added b-sides and 'Dart (demo)', in a digipak with liner notes by Steve Bell and Andrew Stafford.

Poison City Records, 2014 – vinyl gatefold.

Poison City Records/Modern Morning 2022 – vinyl gatefold.

Compilations

7 Year Glitch (Hypnotised, 1996)

Closing Alaska (Guilt Ridden Pop, 1997) – this US-released CD EP compiles tracks from Kitten Licks and Fill Yourself with Music along with 'Early Talker', a b-side from the 'Static' single.

Introducing: Screamfeeder. Singles & More 1992–2004 (Shock, 2004)

Cargo Embargo (Self-released, 2011)

All the Other Times: A Pop Guilt Companion (Rogue Wave Records, 2017)

Patterns Form (Four Four/ABC Music/Universal Music, 2018)

Notes

Chapter 1

1   Stratton (2006).

2   The quote is taken from Andrew Stafford's 2004 scene history *Pig City: From the Saints to Savage Garden* (University of Queensland Press).

Chapter 2

1   Toowoomba is just over 100 km inland from Brisbane, on the crest of the Great Dividing Range in the Darling Downs farming region. It is one of Queensland's largest regional centres and one of Australia's most populous inland cities, passing 100,000 residents in the 1980s.

2   The 'Target building', a multi-storey former department store between the two central pedestrian malls in Fortitude Valley, was decrepit and maze-like in the early 1990s when it was used as a rehearsal space by bands including Screamfeeder, Custard, Hateman, Pangaea and Powderfinger. In 2003, the century-old building was listed on the Queensland Heritage Register as the TC Beirne Complex and Fortuneland Centre, and it now holds a retail arcade, apartments and offices. Mount Coot-tha, approximately 6 km west of the Brisbane CBD, is the site of the Brisbane Botanic Gardens and a lookout from the city's highest summit.

3 Mackay is a coastal port city between central and north Queensland, almost 1,000 km north of Brisbane, with a population passing 60,000 in the late 1980s. Located near the Whitsunday Islands and Great Barrier Reef, it has transitioned from Australia's sugar capital to a coal mining gateway.

4 Tewantin is a rural town in the Sunshine Coast region, around 130 km north of Brisbane.

5 Townsville, the unofficial capital of north Queensland, is a coastal city more than 1,300km from Brisbane (and more than four hours' drive from Mackay), with a population under 100,000 in the mid-1980s. As well as being a regional administrative hub, the city is a national defence base and an industrial centre for mineral processing and exports.

6 Taken from the *Dig Me Out* podcast, Episode 121 – Tim Steward of Screamfeeder. See Minneci, T. and Dizak, J. (2013).

7 Taken from *The Ending Goes Forever* podcast, Episode 2 – Flour: Metal On Metal, October 2022.

8 Taken from the liner notes of the 2014 vinyl reissue of *Flour* on Poison City Records. See *Selected Discography*.

9 Ibid.

10 *Pig City: From the Saints to Savage Garden:* 226.

11 From *Some of My Best Work* podcast, April 2022.

12 *The Ending Goes Forever* podcast, ep 3.

13 Taken from the liner notes of the 2014 vinyl reissue of *Burn Out Your Name* on Poison City Records. See *Selected Discography*.

14 rooArt was a record label founded in 1988 by INXS manager Chris Murphy, with funding and distribution by major label Polygram. By the time of this meeting, Warner Music had acquired half of the company and taken over distribution

(Shoebridge, 1993). For more detail on rooArt, Chris Murphy and Todd Wagstaff see Mathieson (2000).

15 From *Some of My Best Work* podcast, April 2022.

16 Interview with Claire Sutchberry on *Firewater*, PBS radio, 26 April 2022.

Chapter 3

1 Sludgy Brisbane metal band Hateman were one of the heaviest bands in their local 90s grunge/alternative cohort, and certainly one of the most intimidating live. They released a single full-length album via Fellaheen – 1994's *Triple Forte* – before disbanding. While Hateman was a dramatically different project to Screamfeeder, the era both bands worked in was defined by heavy guitar rock and Brisbane's small music scenes led to a significant amount of creative cross pollination. Screamfeeder's social circle also featured heavier, metal-tinged acts such as Midget, Tweezer and Budd. Additionally, Tim and Kellie played in side-project Slugfest (with members of Budd), a much heavier outfit.

2 From Borg, *The Complete Recordings Of Tim Steward (1987–2015)*, Appendix C.

3 Ibid.

Chapter 4

1 Today, Rockinghorse Studios offers onsite accommodation. In 1996, Screamfeeder stayed at a house some kilometres away, past the village of Federal.

2   Darek Mudge is Screamfeeder's other guitarist, 2001–2005 and 2014–present.

3   Borg, *The Complete Recordings Of Tim Steward (1987–2015)*, Appendix C.

4   Harmonics are amplified overtones sounded by a guitar or bass guitar. They're typically created by very lightly fretting a string and striking it, thus producing a high-pitched tone that is not the fundamental of that fret position, but a harmonic accompanying sound.

Chapter 5

1   The Triple J Hottest 100 is an annual radio listener poll, ranking the most popular tracks of the year. In 1996, 'Buy Me A Pony' by Screamfeeder contemporary (and touring partner) Spiderbait was the first Australian track voted in at number 1.

2   Interview in *Puretest* zine, 1998.

3   From Darren Levin's review in *Mess + Noise*, 2009.

Chapter 6

1   Email interview from *Puretest* zine, 1998.

2   Interview in *Pee* zine #13.

3   Email interview from *Puretest* zine, 1998.

4   Interview in *Pee* zine #13.

5   *Beat Magazine* interview, 1998.

6   Mathieson (2000) details how Ratcat's rapid 'crossover' from the Sydney punk scene to the top of the charts in 1991 gained them a new, but ultimately fickle audience and alienated their previous one, damaging their longevity. Joe Segreto was Ratcat's manager.

7   Taken from the liner notes of the *Patterns Form* compilation. See *Selected Discography*.

Chapter 7

1   From press release for *Kitten Licks* twenty-fifth anniversary concert.

2   From Darren Levin's review in *Mess + Noise*, 2009.

3   From Ian Rogers's interview in *The Vine*, 2009.

List of References

Borg, C. (2016) *The Complete Recordings of Tim Steward (1987–2015)*. Moonlight Publications. Available at: https://ozmusicbooks.com/product/the-complete-recordings-of-tim-steward-1987-2015/

Grimson, T. (1996) 'Kitten Licks – Screamfeeder'. *Rolling Stone* magazine, September.

Levin, D. (2009) 'Kitten Licks (Record Reviews)'. *Mess + Noise.* Available at: https://screamfeeder.com/wp-content/uploads/2010/03/Screamfeeder-Kitten-Licks-on-MandN.pdf

Mathieson, C. (2000) *The Sell-In: How the Music Business Seduced Alternative Rock*. Allen & Unwin.

Minneci, T. and Dizak, J. (2013) *Dig Me Out*: #121 Tim Steward of Screamfeeder [Podcast] https://www.digmeoutpodcast.com/episode/121-interview-with-tim-steward-of-screamfeeder

Pee (1999) [Fanzine], no. 13, Self-published zine.

Puretest (1998) [Fanzine] May, Self-published zine.

Recovery (1997) [TV programme] ABC, 4 October

Rogers, I. (2009) 'Interview – Screamfeeder'. *The Vine*. Available at: http://screamfeeder.com/wp-content/uploads/2010/03/Interview-Screamfeeder-the-vine.pdf

Rogers, I. (2012). 'Musicians and Aspiration: Exploring the Rock Dream in Independent Music', PhD thesis, School of English, Media Studies and Art History, University of Queensland, Brisbane.

Screamfeeder (2022) *End of This Summer*. Available at: www.screamfeeder.com

Shoebridge, N. (1993) 'The Sultan of Synergy'. *Australian Financial Review*, 28 May. Available at: https://www.afr.com/companies/the-sultan-of-synergy-19930528-kaqug

Smoking Dog Press (1996) [Fanzine], no. 2, Self-published zine.

Some of My Best Work (2022) [Podcast], 'Tim Steward – Wrote You Off (Screamfeeder)'. Mushroom Group, April.

Stafford, A. (1995) 'New Vibrations: The Beach Boys haunt Screamfeeder'. *Rolling Stone* magazine, July: 25.

Stafford, A. (2004) *Pig City: From the Saints to Savage Garden*. University of Queensland Press.

Stratton, J. (2006) 'Nation Building and Australian Popular Music in the 1970s and 1980s'. *Continuum: Journal of Media and Cultural Studies* 20(2): 243–52.

Sutchberry, C. (2022) *Firewater*, PBS radio 106.7fm, 26 April.

The Ending Goes Forever (2022), [Podcast] Patreon.

Acknowledgements

We sincerely thank Tim, Kellie and Dean for their support for this book, without which it would not have been possible, and their cooperation including lengthy interviews, assistance finding people and documents, and fact-checking. We hope we have done justice to the stories you so generously shared. Thanks to Joe Woolley for his in-depth interview and assistance with organisation and documents. Thanks to everyone who participated in an interview or shared their memories in writing: Steve Bell, Alex Campbell, Kate Cooper, Andy Hayden, Damien Hughes, Kellie Lloyd, Kate McGuire, Paul McKercher, Darek Mudge, John Scott, Andrew P. Street, Seja Vogel and Chris Yates. Thanks to Freya Langley for interview transcription. Thanks to Stephen Booth for photographs from the recording session and Carl Breitkreuz for permission to reproduce his illustrations. Thanks to the Oceania series editors, especially Jon Stratton for his careful reading and advice, and Leah Babb-Rosenfeld of Bloomsbury Publishing. Thanks to the anonymous peer reviewers for their feedback on the original proposal. Research for this book, especially with regard to historical press coverage of the band and album, was aided by the Tim Steward/Screamfeeder archive held by the State Library of Queensland.

Index